Table of Contents

Practice Test #1

Practice Questions

Scientific Concepts

1. In general, antibiotics will kill which type of infection?
    a. Bacterial
    b. Viral
    c. Parasitic
    d. All of the above

2. Which of the following is correct about Safety Data Sheets (SDS)?
    a. They include fire-fighting measures but not first-aid measures.
    b. They cover ecological information required by the OSHA's HCS.
    c. They cover identifying hazardous materials but not the hazards.
    d. They include measures for accidental release but not exposure.

3. Flushing thoroughly with water for at least 15-20 minutes is a common first aid measure for...
    a. Minor wounds to the skin.
    b. Minor chemical skin burns.
    c. Minor chemical eye burns.
    d. Minor wounds of all types.

4. Which of the following organelles in human cells turn food into energy?
    a. The vacuoles
    b. The lysosomes
    c. The ribosomes
    d. The mitochondria

5. Which type of tissue is found most abundantly in the human body?
    a. Nervous tissue
    b. Muscular tissue
    c. Epithelial tissue
    d. Connective tissue

6. Which part(s) of the heart pump(s) blood from the heart to the body?
    a. The atria
    b. The valves
    c. The ventricles
    d. The pericardium

7. Which of the following normally keep(s) people from inhaling foods and liquids?
    a. The esophagus
    b. The epiglottis
    c. The trachea
    d. The bronchi

8. In which layer of the skin are collagen bundles located?
   a. The basal layer
   b. The epidermis
   c. The subcutis
   d. The dermis

9. In the skull, which are cranial bones that come in pairs?
   a. The frontal and occipital bones
   b. The sphenoid and ethmoid bones
   c. The parietal and temporal bones
   d. The zygomatic and maxillary bones

10. Which of the following bones are found in the neck?
   a. Thoracic vertebrae
   b. Cervical vertebrae
   c. Lumbar vertebrae
   d. All of the above

11. Of the following, which shoulder bone connects the arm to the trunk?
   a. The clavicle
   b. The humerus
   c. The scapula
   d. All of the above

12. The carpal bones are found in the…
   a. Forearm.
   b. Wrist.
   c. Hand.
   d. Fingers.

13. Which two leg bones connect to form the knee joint?
   a. The tibia and the fibula
   b. The femur and the fibula
   c. The femur and the tibia
   d. The tarsal and calcaneus

14. Which of the following muscles is found under the top of the scalp?
   a. The mentalis muscle
   b. The occipitalis muscle
   c. The frontalis muscle
   d. Galea aponeurotica

15. The "kissing" sphincter muscle circling the mouth is called…
   a. Zygomaticus major.
   b. Zygomaticus minor.
   c. The orbicularis oris.
   d. Platysma muscle.

16. Which eye muscles are responsible for rolling the eyes in circular directions?
    a. The superior and inferior rectus muscles
    b. The superior and inferior oblique muscles
    c. The lateral and medial rectus eye muscles
    d. All of the above work together in rolling the eyes

17. The vestibulo-ocular system that comprises the complex of eye movements functions through coordination of the eyes and the _____ when the head and body are moving.
    a. Inner ear
    b. Middle ear
    c. Forehead
    d. Cranium

18. Among the arm muscles, the biceps are _____ and the triceps are _____.
    a. Extensors; flexors
    b. Flexors; extensors
    c. Adductors; abductors
    d. Abductors; adductors

19. The movements of human fingers are primarily controlled by powerful muscles in the...
    a. Wrists.
    b. Hands.
    c. Forearms.
    d. Palms.

20. Among the muscles involved in enabling human legs and feet to walk, which is the strongest?
    a. Hamstring muscles
    b. The biceps femoris
    c. The adductor longus
    d. The gluteus maximus

21. In effect, the shoulder muscles include which of the following?
    a. The pectoral muscles in the chest
    b. The trapezius in the neck and back
    c. Muscle groups attached to the ribs
    d. All of the above and more

22. Which type of joint allows a person's thumb to cross the palms of his or her hand?
    a. Ball-and-socket
    b. A gliding joint
    c. A saddle joint
    d. A hinge joint

23. The lymphatic system performs which of the following functions?
    a. Transporting fluids from the circulatory system to the tissues
    b. Transporting fluids from the tissues to the circulatory system
    c. Transporting fatty acids from foods into the digestive system
    d. Transporting lymph via its vessels away from lymphatic ducts

24. Which of the following organs is a part of the respiratory system?
    a. These all are
    b. The mouth
    c. The larynx
    d. The pharynx

25. The _____ nervous system includes the brain and spinal cord, while the _____ nervous system includes the sense organs, nerves, and other parts.
    a. Peripheral; central
    b. Central; peripheral
    c. Autonomic; enteric
    d. Somatic; autonomic

26. Which of the following should a cosmetologist do to keep body positioning ergonomic and avoid straining his/her joints and muscles while working?
    a. Keep a very tight grip on the implements or tools
    b. Reach across the table whenever giving manicures
    c. Hold the arms close to the body while working
    d. Bend the wrists up and down often in using tools

27. Chemicals with a _____ pH are acid, like lemon juice and vinegar; chemicals with a _____ pH are alkaline, like ammonia, laundry soap, and lye.
    a. Neutral; reactive
    b. Basic; neutral
    c. High; low
    d. Low; high

28. The opposite of a generic medication is...
    a. An over-the-counter medication.
    b. A non-prescription medication.
    c. A prescription medication.
    d. A patented medication.

29. In circuits of electrical current, the particles that carry a charge through wires are called...
    a. Protons.
    b. Electrons.
    c. Neutrons.
    d. Amperes.

30. In cosmetology, which of the following is a common use of light therapy?
    a. Treating hyperpigmentation
    b. Treating wrinkles and loose skin
    c. Treating any and all of these
    d Treating acne (antibacterial)

Hair Care and Services

31. Which of the following is the order of the layers in a hair shaft, from innermost to outermost?
    a. Cuticle, cortex, medulla
    b. Cortex, cuticle, medulla
    c. Cuticle, medulla, cortex
    d. Medulla, cortex, cuticle

32. In which order do the cell layers of the inner root sheath (IRS) of a hair and cells of the hair cuticle keratinize (i.e., form through the conversion and hardening of skin cells), from first to last?
    a. Innermost/IRS cuticle layer, middle/Huxley layer, cuticle cells, outermost/Henle layer
    b. Innermost/IRS cuticle layer, cuticle cells, middle/Huxley layer, outermost/Henle layer
    c. Outermost/Henle layer, innermost/IRS cuticle layer, cuticle cells, middle/Huxley layer
    d. Outermost/Henle layer, middle/Huxley layer, cuticle cells, innermost/IRS cuticle layer

33. If someone's hair is extremely porous, it will _____ moisture.
    a. Absorb and hold
    b. Absorb and lose
    c. Retain but repel
    d. Repel plus lose

34. Human hair growth has three stages, or phases. Which of the following phases lasts for the longest time, and involves the most hairs on the head at any one time?
    a. The anagen or the growth phase
    b. The catagen or transitional phase
    c. The telogen or the resting phase
    d. None of these has both qualities

35. If hair seems to have developed a tolerance to a certain shampoo and no longer shows the same benefits from the product as before, what should be done?
    a. Switch to another shampoo permanently
    b. Change to another shampoo temporarily
    c. Try using the shampoo more or less often
    d. Nothing; tolerance to shampoo is a myth

36. A client has a "moon face" that she wants to minimize. Which hairstyle would best do this?
    a. A lot of volume, making the face appear smaller by contrast
    b. A short, curly hairstyle to balance out the face's roundness
    c. A little top volume, sleek on the sides, and past chin-length
    d. A very short haircut that will not add to the size of her face

37. Rollers are used to set the hair in...
    a. Thermal styling.
    b. Wet-set styling.
    c. Permanent styling.
    d. Any or all of the above

38. Which method of attaching hair extensions is most likely to involve tightly braiding or cornrowing the client's original hair?
    a. Clipping in the extensions
    b. Gluing in the extensions
    c. Sewing in the extensions
    d. All of these involve braiding

39. When a person grows old, his or her rate of hair growth can typically slow down to…
    a. One inch per month.
    b. One-tenth of an inch per month.
    c. A half-inch per month.
    d. Eight-tenths of an inch per month.

40. On the average person with a healthy scalp, a full head of hair has around _____ hairs.
    a. 100,000
    b. 10,000
    c. 1 million
    d. 20,000

41. Under normal conditions, how many hairs does a healthy, non-balding person lose every day?
    a. About 50
    b. About 100
    c. About 25
    d. About 200

42. Which of the following is a difference between dandruff and dry scalp?
    a. Dry scalp has more redness, irritation, and odor.
    b. It is believed that an infection causes a dry scalp.
    c. Dandruff causes larger, often greasy skin flakes.
    d. There is no difference; they are the same thing.

43. Which of the following is a common treatment for dandruff?
    a. Scalp steaming or warm, moist towel wraps
    b. Applying deep conditioning scalp treatments
    c. Scalp massages or salon high-frequency D.C.
    d. OTC-medicated shampoos and conditioners

44. Brushing the hair thoroughly and massaging the scalp is helpful for which scalp condition?
    a. Oily scalp
    b. Dry scalp
    c. A and B
    d. None of the above

45. When someone has acne on the scalp, which kind of treatment for it should be avoided?
    a. Salicylic acid
    b. Benzoyl peroxide
    c. Oily scalp shampoo
    d. An astringent lotion

46. What is most accurate about hair capes that stylists/salons can buy to protect clients' clothes?
    a. Rotating use of several cheaper capes will make them last as long as or longer than pricier ones.
    b. Hairstylists/salons should always buy more expensive capes as they last longer than cheap ones.
    c. Hair capes made for shampooing and chemical treatments are more expensive and are heavier.
    d. Hair capes made for styling offer better protection against liquids dripping through onto clothes.

47. Which kind of material is the best in a hair cape to be used for cutting hair?
    a. A cape of rough-textured fabric
    b. A slippery synthetic styling cape
    c. A hair cape made out of plastic
    d. A fabric cape should be avoided

48. Which of the following is true about massaging the scalp during shampooing?
    a. It inhibits the circulation of blood to the hair follicles.
    b. It limits the supply of nutrients and oils to hair shafts.
    c. It generates better tips for the shampoo attendants.
    d. It should always be done using larger finger motions.

49. The cleansing agents in shampoo are called...
    a. None of these.
    b. Hydrophilics.
    c. Lipophilics.
    d. Surfactants.

50. What is the best general rule for how often to shampoo the hair?
    a. Shampoo the hair every day
    b. Shampoo hair twice a week
    c. Shampoo when hair is dirty
    d. Shampoo only once a week

51. What kind of technique helps create a hairstyle that curves under at the ends?
    a. Overcutting
    b. Undercutting
    c. Outer layering
    d. Short top layers

52. Which of the following makes it easiest to detect the growth pattern of hair on the crown or back of the head?
    a. Air-drying one's hair first
    b. Blow-drying the hair first
    c. Looking at it with mirrors
    d. A friend, not a hairstylist

53. What is true if a person has both curly and straight hair without styling it that way?
    a. Only environmental stress causes this.
    b. Many people have this growth pattern.
    c. This never happens on the same head.
    d. This is only due to a rare genetic defect.

54. Which natural hair color is the densest in terms of number of hairs per square inch?
    a. Red
    b. Black
    c. Blond
    d. Brown

55. What kind of hairstyle is generally more flattering on an overweight person?
    a. An overall short hairstyle
    b. An overall "big" hairstyle
    c. More horizontal volume
    d. Medium vertical volume

56. Which statement is most accurate about cutting a man's hair using clippers to taper the sides?
    a. Clippers-over-comb cutting is easy without experience.
    b. Clipper attachments have uniform-length teeth for this.
    c. Clipper attachments using angled combs are the safest.
    d. Clipper attachments are shortest for the top of the hair.

57. A client with naturally fine, thin hair requests an extremely "big" hairdo. Which of the following recommendations should a stylist make that would be the most realistic?
    a. A perm for volume, strong styling gel, jumbo rollers, teasing, and lots of hairspray
    b. Products and styling can add volume for a fuller look, but it will never be that "big"
    c. Tell the client this is impossible and recommend a cute, very short haircut instead
    d. Advise the client that if "big" hair is a must, the only styling option is to buy a wig

58. When hairstylists refer to angles in cutting hair, this means that cutting the hair at a certain angle involves holding the scissors at an angle relative to...
    a. The floor.
    b. The hairs.
    c. The hand.
    d. The face.

59. In terms of the areas of the head that pertain to haircutting, which area is the second highest on the head, directly below the top of the head?
    a. The occipital bone
    b. The parietal ridges
    c. The head's crown
    d. The temple areas

60. When giving a graduated haircut, the stylist brings the hair ends at both sides together in the front or the back to see if they meet in the center. This is called...
    a. Over-direction.
    b. Hair-sectioning.
    c. Cross-checking.
    d. Back-combing.

61. How many sections are the standard to divide the hair into before cutting it?
    a. Four
    b. Five
    c. Six
    d. Seven

62. Which of the following is most accurate about the terms "graduated" and "layered" for haircuts?
    a. Graduated haircuts do not have layers.
    b. Layered haircuts are never graduated.
    c. Graduated cuts have more even layers.
    d. Layered cuts include more even layers.

63. In general, which of the following is most accurate regarding braids on children?
    a. Braids are always complicated and time-consuming to fashion.
    b. Simple braids can be quickly made on children by busy parents.
    c. Braids on children will not stay in shape as long as other styles.
    d. Braided hair on children is more likely to tangle, snarl, or mat.

64. Which is true about how to tell if a wig is made of natural or synthetic hair?
    a. Pull out a strand and burn it: real hair burns slowly, with a certain smell.
    b. Pull out a strand and burn it: synthetic hair gives off a much worse odor.
    c. Pull out a strand and burn it: real hair burns faster while synthetic melts.
    d. Pull out a strand and burn it: real hair balls up, synthetic burns out faster.

65. When should a skin patch test be made on a client?
    a. Before coloring, but not perms or straightening
    b. Before performing any and all chemical services
    c. To test coloring formulas but not the developers
    d. 8-12 hours before any planned chemical service

66. Which of the following kinds of chemical permanent wave solutions have the highest pH?
    a. Acid waves
    b. Acid-balanced
    c. Cold waves
    d. Sulfite-based

67. A common complaint of clients with brunette hair color is that "it has too much red in it." According to the laws of color, what color will cancel out too much red?
    a. Blue
    b. Yellow
    c. Violet
    d. Green

68. A temporary hair color rinse typically will last...
    a. For about eight to 12 shampoos.
    b. For about two or three shampoos.
    c. For about four to six shampoos.
    d. Until the next shampoo.

69. Which kind(s) of hair color can lighten the hair's natural color?
    a. Semi-permanent color
    b. Demi-permanent color
    c. A permanent hair color
    d. They all can lighten hair

70. A client with naturally dark brown hair and some gray hairs used a hair color at home. She chose a lighter golden-brown tint, thinking it would color the gray hairs to create golden-brown highlights. Unfortunately, she did not realize that not being a deposit-only color, it instead lightened all her hair to a uniform lighter brown that she does not like. Which of the following would be best for a color correction?
    a. Use foils to bleach some strands into highlights after coloring.
    b. Use foils to protect selected strands and color the rest darker.
    c. Color all of the hair darker and tell her to do without highlights.
    d. Strip all of the color from all of the hair and start all over again.

Skin Care and Services

71. Which layer of the skin is connective tissue made mainly of collagen?
    a. Dermis
    b. Epidermis
    c. Hypodermis
    d. Stratum corneum

72. Which kinds of glands in the skin are most associated with the hair follicles?
    a. Eccrine
    b. Apocrine
    c. Sebaceous
    d. Tubular glands

73. The following factors all contribute to skin color. Which of them is a pigment?
    a. Dermis
    b. Melanin
    c. Collagen
    d. Hemoglobin

74. Which type of skin cancer is both the least common and the most dangerous?
    a. Melanoma
    b. Basal cell carcinoma
    c. Squamous cell carcinoma
    d. No cancer has this combination

75. When a cosmetologist does an initial skin analysis for a client, with which skin condition is s/he most likely to avoid using much steam and/or pressure?
    a. Acne
    b. Rosacea
    c. Blackheads
    d. Whiteheads

76. Which of the following should be included for proper draping of a client during a facial treatment?
    a. A cape
    b. A towel
    c. A hairband
    d. All of the above

77. Which type of tweezers are recommended for general eyebrow shaping?
    a. Pointed-tip tweezers
    b. Square-tip tweezers
    c. Slanted-tip tweezers
    d. This does not matter

78. Which of the following is true about threading as a hair removal method?
    a. Threading is a very new method.
    b. Threading is less painful than wax.
    c. Threading does not pull out hairs.
    d. Threading is permanent removal.

79. Regarding sugaring as a method of removing hair, which of the following is accurate?
    a. Sugaring can be gentler than waxing.
    b. Sugaring is a fairly recent innovation.
    c. Sugaring uses all-chemical ingredients.
    d. Sugaring is limited to Western culture.

80. Before working on each client, all cosmetology instruments must be…
    a. Cleansed thoroughly through the use of soap and water.
    b. Immersed in an EPA-registered bactericidal disinfectant.
    c. Immersed in a disinfectant that is fungicidal and virucidal.
    d. All of the above

81. Which of the following is true about electric facials?
    a. They are used to plump and activate facial muscles.
    b. They are used to slim the face by removing the fat.
    c. They are used to give current equal to a light bulb's.
    d. They are used to stop wrinkles via muscle paralysis.

82. What statement is most accurate regarding topical creams used as dermal fillers versus injections?
    a. There is no topical cream that works as a filler.
    b. Some topical products do provide filler effects.
    c. Topical fillers have no benefits over injections.
    d. Topical fillers are all the same and widely used.

83. Adding black to a hue or true color will produce a _____ of that color.
    a. Tint
    b. Tone
    c. Shade
    d. Value

84. Among the following, which would be the least likely to be specialty makeup?
    a. Makeup that an actor wears onstage for a theatrical play
    b. Makeup used to create monsters in movies or TV shows
    c. Makeup a person wears to a Halloween costume party
    d. Makeup an office employee wears to work every day

85. Why is it important to get a patch test before applying false eyelashes?
    a. In case of any allergies to the adhesive
    b. In case of any allergies to lash material
    c. For every reason in all of these choices
    d. To protect cosmetologists from liability

Nail Care and Services

86. Human fingernails and toenails are made out of...
    a. Perionychium.
    b. Hyponychium.
    c. Eponychium.
    d. Keratin.

87. Which of the following fingernail conditions can be caused by the skin condition psoriasis?
    a. Nail pitting
    b. Separation
    c. (A) and (B)
    d. Spoon nails

88. Human fingernails take an average of _____ for total regrowth, while human toenails take an average of _____.
    a. 6-12 months; 6-12 months
    b. 3-6 months; 12-18 months
    c. 12-18 months; 6-9 months
    d. 6-9 months; 18-24 months

89. Terry's nails refers to a condition wherein each fingernail has a dark band just below the white nail tip. Which of the following is true about this condition?
    a. It can sometimes be due to aging.
    b. It is always caused by liver disease.
    c. It is never related to heart failure.
    d. It is associated only with diabetes.

90. Thickened, yellow nails can be signs of yellow nail syndrome. What is correct about this syndrome?
    a. This is a name for, and is caused by, nail fungus.
    b. This can be associated with a chronic bronchitis.
    c. This has no known connection to lymphedema.
    d. This will not cause separation or affect cuticles.

91. Among nail care tools, which might not have to be thrown away after use on a client?
    a. Cotton balls and/or pads
    b. Emery boards might not
    c. Certain kinds of nail files
    d. All of the above can be saved

92. For shaping the nails, what number of grit is recommended to use?
    a. At least 80
    b. Above 3600
    c. 180 is enough
    d. Finer than 240

93. Many nail technicians would rather use which tool(s) to remove extra cuticle from the nails?
    a. A cuticle pusher is sufficient
    b. A cuticle nipper and a curette
    c. A curette replaces the others
    d. All three should go together

94. For which clients are hot oil manicures always recommended?
    a. Clients with very dry nails
    b. Both (A) and (C), not (D)
    c. Clients with very dry skin
    d. For manicuring all clients

95. What is advised in using pedicure tubs when giving pedicures to elderly clients?
    a. To use tubs with massaging machines
    b. To use very hot water for soaking feet
    c. To avoid (A) and (B) for elderly clients
    d. To consult a doctor is never necessary

96. When are cosmetologists prohibited by law from giving a client massage?
    a. If the client has athlete's foot
    b. When the client has eczema
    c. If the client has inflamed skin/eruptions
    d. They are prohibited in any of these cases

97. When massaging the hands and arms, which of the following should be avoided?
    a. Gently twisting and pulling the fingers
    b. Pressing between back wrist bones
    c. None of these should be avoided
    d. Massaging the base of the thumb

98. When setting up a manicure table before performing nail care, which of the following is the correct order for the first five steps of pre-service procedures?
    a. Wrap the arm cushion in a sanitized towel; clean the table; put clean implements in the disinfectant container; fill the container 20 minutes before the first manicure; place products on the table.
    b. Clean the table; wrap the arm cushion in a sanitized towel; fill the disinfectant container 20 minutes before the first manicure; put clean implements in the container; place products on the table.
    c. Fill the disinfectant container 20 minutes before the first manicure; clean the table; wrap the arm cushion in a sanitized towel; put clean implements in the container; place products on the table.
    d. Put clean implements in the disinfectant container; fill the container 20 minutes before the first manicure; wrap the arm cushion in a sanitized towel; clean the table; place products on the table.

99. Which of the following is true about applying nail tips?
    a. The nail tip should cover less than half of the natural nail.
    b. The nail tip should cover more than half of the natural nail.
    c. The nail tips can add durability and strength to nail overlays.
    d. The nail tips are blended by filing, including the natural nails.

100. Which of the following is true about gel nails as opposed to acrylic nails?
    a. Gel nails cure with air exposure like acrylics, but take longer to cure.
    b. Gel nails tend to create a more natural appearance than acrylic nails.
    c. Gel nails must be filed off and can never be soaked off like acrylics.
    d. Gel nails are more expensive than acrylic nails, but they last longer.

Answers and Explanations

Scientific Concepts

1. A: In general, antibiotics kill bacteria and the infections they cause. Antibiotics will not cure infections caused by viruses (B). Some viruses, like the common cold virus, mutate so frequently that no agent has been found to kill them. Other viruses, like influenza, do mutate but less often, so they can often be prevented via immunization (such as flu shots). Parasitic (C) infections must be prevented or treated with other medications. A few medications, like metronidazole (e.g., brand names oral Flagyl and topical Metrogel), kill both bacteria and parasites. Thus, choice (D) is incorrect.

2. B: The Hazard Communication Standards (HCS) given by the OSHA (Occupational Safety and Health Administration) require certain information to be included in SDS. However, the 16-section format that the OSHA recommends for SDS includes ecological information that is NOT required by its HCS. This format includes both fire-fighting and first-aid measures (A), identification of hazardous materials and also of the hazards themselves (C), and measures both for accidental release of hazardous materials and for personal protection and control of exposure (D) to hazardous materials in the workplace.

3. C: For minor chemical burns to the eyes, a common first aid measure is to flush the eyes with plain water for at least 15-20 minutes. Common first aid measures for minor skin wounds (A) include cleaning the wound with warm, soapy water (but not flushing for 15-20 minutes). For minor chemical skin burns (B), common first aid measures include cleaning the burn with cool, soapy water (but not flushing for 15-20 minutes). Therefore, option (D) is incorrect.

4. D: The mitochondria are the cell organelles that provide power by converting nutrients into energy. The vacuoles (A) are the cell organelles that store water, food, and waste until these are utilized or eliminated. The lysosomes (B) are the cell organelles that break down proteins, sugars, and some fats. The ribosomes (C) are the cell organelles that form proteins.

5. D: Connective tissue is the most abundant type of tissue in the human body. It binds together the body structures as well as performing other functions. Nerve tissue (A) is found in the brain, the nerves, and the spinal cord. Muscular tissue (B) is found in the voluntary skeletal muscles, in hollow organs like the stomach, and in the heart wall. Epithelial tissue (C) covers all inner and outer body surfaces, is the primary glandular tissue, and attaches to the connective tissue underneath it, but it is not as abundant in the body as connective tissue.

6. C: The ventricles, or the two lower chambers of the heart, pump blood to the body. The atria (A), or the two upper chambers of the heart, receive blood coming back from the body to the heart. The heart's valves (B) open and close to let blood flow in a single direction between the heart's chambers. The pericardium (D) is the fluid-filled sac that surrounds the heart.

7. B: The epiglottis separates the esophagus (A), through which people swallow foods and liquids, from the trachea (C) or windpipe, through which people breathe. The bronchi (D) are the two breathing tubes into which the trachea divides at the left and right to lead to each lung.

8. D: The dermis is the middle layer of the skin, containing collagen bundles, blood and lymph vessels, sweat glands, hair follicles, nerves, and fibroblasts. The basal layer (A) is the deepest layer

of the epidermis (B), which is the outermost layer of the skin. The subcutis (C), or subcutaneous layer, is the innermost layer of the skin.

9. C: The parietal and temporal bones come in pairs, one on each side of the skull (cranium). The frontal and occipital bones (A) are unpaired; the frontal is at the front and the occipital at the rear of the skull. The sphenoid and ethmoid bones (B) are also unpaired: each of these single bones runs through the mid-sagittal plane and helps to connect the cranial and facial bones. The zygomatic and maxillary bones (D) do come in pairs, but they are facial bones, not cranial bones.

10. B: The cervical vertebrae are the bones of the upper spine found in the neck. The thoracic vertebrae (A) are the bones of the middle spine that articulate (connect) with the ribcage. The lumbar vertebrae (C) are the bones of the lower spine found in the lower back. Therefore, option (D) is incorrect because only the cervical vertebrae are found in the neck.

11. A: The clavicle, or collarbone, is the only shoulder bone that connects between the arm and trunk. The humerus (B) is the shoulder bone found in the upper arm. The scapula (C) is the bone of the shoulder blade, found in the back. The humerus and scapula do not attach between the trunk and arm, making choice (D) incorrect.

12. B: The wrist contains eight carpal bones. The forearm (A) contains the bones known as the radius and the ulna. The hand (C) contains five metacarpal bones. The fingers (D) and thumb contain 14 small bones known as phalanges.

13. C: The femur, or thigh bone, connects with the tibia, or shin bone, to form the knee joint. The fibula {(A), (B)} is the other long lower-leg bone in addition to the tibia. The fibula functions more for muscle attachments than leg support, and forms a part of the ankle joint. The tarsal bones are found in the ankle, and the calcaneus is the heel bone (D).

14. D: The galea aponeurotica is the muscle found at the top of the head. It connects with the occipitalis (B) muscle (or occipital belly of the epicranius muscle) at the back of the head and the frontalis (C) muscle (or frontal belly of the epicranius muscle) at the front of the head or forehead to pull back the scalp, wrinkle the forehead, and raise the eyebrows. The mentalis muscle (A) is found in the chin.

15. C: The orbicularis oris muscle is a sphincter surrounding the mouth between the nose and chin. The zygomaticus major (B) and zygomaticus minor (B) muscles are in the cheek area, forming the nasolabial furrows between nose and mouth and help to articulate the mouth, nose, and cheeks. The platysma (D) is a larger muscle along the neck's sides between the shoulder and collarbone, which also controls downward and sideways movement of the mouth and lower lip to open the mouth partially.

16. B: The superior and inferior oblique muscles in the eyes work to roll the eyes in clockwise and counterclockwise directions. There are three pairs of eye muscles; within each pair, each muscle works in opposition to the other, balancing each other's pull on the eye. The superior and inferior rectus muscles (A) work to roll the eyes backward and upward, and forward and downward. The lateral and medial rectus muscles (C) pull the eyes outward away from the nose, and inward toward the nose. Therefore, choice (D) is also incorrect because only the superior and inferior oblique muscles work to roll the eyes in circular directions.

17. A: The vestibular system is in the inner ear and controls the sense of balance. When the head and/or body are moving, the movements of the eyes keep images on rodless parts of the retina, coordinating with information about the head's movements provided to the brain by the vestibular system. This complex is called the vestibulo-ocular system. The vestibular system is not in the middle ear (B) or forehead (C). The cranium (D) is the skull, which contains the eyes, middle ear, inner ear, and many other structures.

18. B: The biceps in the fronts of the upper arms are flexor muscles, which contract; the triceps in the backs of the upper arms are extensor muscles, which extend. These work in opposition to provide flexibility for complex arm movements, including shoulder and elbow joint movements. Abductors are muscles that move limbs away from the body's midline, whereas adductors are muscles that move limbs toward the midline {(C), (D)}; for example, with the arms, hips, and legs.

19. C: When muscles in the forearms contract, they pull on attached tendons to bend the fingers. Tendons in the wrists (A) help the hands as well as the wrists to articulate. Tendons along the fingers are encased in sheaths on the palm (D) sides of the hands. Extrinsic hand muscles also aid in flexing and extending the hands and fingers. While intrinsic hand (C) muscles supply precise coordination of fine-motor finger movements, the primary sources of control of human fingers are the strong muscles in the forearms.

20. D: The gluteus maximus is not only the strongest walking muscle but also the strongest muscle in the entire body. Found in the buttocks, the gluteus maximus straightens the leg at the hip, extends the thigh, and raises the body from a seated to standing posture. The hamstring muscles (A) run behind the back of the thigh and knee and help the knee to flex. The adductor magnus (B) muscle begins at the pelvic bones and inserts to the femur (thigh bone). Its adductor portion moves the hip outward, while its hamstring portion rotates the leg inward. The adductor longus (C) muscle between the pubic bone and femur moves the thigh inward and aids its sideways flexion and rotation.

21. D: In effect, the shoulder muscles include not only the deltoids over the shoulder ball, the rhomboids in the scapula (shoulder blade), and the shoulder itself, but also the pectoral muscles in the chest (A), the trapezius muscle which spreads across the neck, shoulder, and back (B), many groups of small muscles attached to the ribs (C), and to other bones in the skeleton.

22. C: A saddle joint is the type of joint that enables the thumb to cross over the palm. Saddle joints allow movement in two different directions, making them more versatile than hinge or gliding joints. Only ball-and-socket (A) joints have a greater range of motion, as in the shoulder and hip joints. Gliding joints (B) enable movements mainly sideways, albeit a wide range of them; examples are the joint in the upper spine enabling the head to bend and swivel, and the joints that enable the wrists and ankles to twist. Hinge joints (D) are the simplest, usually enabling unidirectional movement as in the elbows, fingers, and toes. (An exception is the knee's hinge joint, which also swivels.)

23. B: The circulation of the lymphatic system carries lymphatic fluids from the body's tissues to the circulatory system, not vice versa (A). Lymphatic circulation transports fatty acids from foods away from the digestive system, not to it (C). Lymph is transported through lymphatic vessels toward, not away from, the lymphatic ducts (D), thence to be moved into the bloodstream.

24. A: These are all parts of the respiratory system, which is composed of all organs that are involved in gas exchanges. These include not only the nose, trachea (windpipe), bronchi, and lungs, but also the mouth (B), the larynx (C), and the pharynx (D).

25. B: The brain and spinal cord make up the central nervous system. The sense organs, nerves, receptors, ganglia—all the parts of the nervous system except the brain and spinal cord—make up the peripheral nervous system. Option (A) has it backwards. The autonomic nervous system is a part of the peripheral nervous system containing the neurons (nerve cells) that control unconscious, involuntary muscular and glandular actions, while the enteric nervous system is a part of the autonomic nervous system that controls the digestive organs and their functions (C). The somatic (D) nervous system is a part of the peripheral nervous system with neurons controlling conscious, voluntary movements of the skeletal muscles, as when people move their bodies and/or body parts.

26. C: A cosmetologist should hold his/her arms close to the body while working because holding the arms away from the body, and/or holding the elbows away from the body at a 60-degree angle or more, will cause joint and muscle strain. Gripping the implements or tools too tightly (A) or squeezing them will also strain the hands and arms. Reaching across the table when giving manicures (B) will cause back strain; it is better to have the client extend an arm across the table so the hand is close enough for the cosmetologist to work on it without reaching. Another thing that causes muscular and joint stress is to bend the wrists up and down all the time when using tools (D), which should be avoided.

27. D: The pH scale goes from 0 to 14. A neutral pH {(A), (B)} is a pH of 7, which pure water has. A pH of 0 to 6 is a low pH. Substances with a low pH are acidic, like lemon juice and vinegar. A pH of 8 to 14 is a high pH. Substances with a high pH are alkaline, like ammonia and laundry detergent. Chemicals that are either extremely acidic or extremely alkaline are reactive (A); for example, battery acid is a reactive acidic chemical, whereas lye is a reactive alkaline chemical. Reactive chemicals can cause severe chemical burns to the skin and eyes. "Basic" (B) is a synonym for alkaline; base or alkali is the opposite of acid. Choice (C) is the reverse of the correct answer.

28. D: Medications are either patented by pharmaceutical manufacturers, giving them exclusive rights to license or make them for up to 20 years; or not patented, i.e., generic. Over-the-counter medications (A) need not be prescribed by a doctor and can be either patented or generic. Non-prescription medications (B) are the same as over-the-counter medications. Prescription medications (C) must be prescribed by a doctor and can be either patented or generic.

29. B: Electrons are negatively charged particles that carry electrical charge through wires in a circuit. Current is the rate at which the charge moves through a circuit, expressed as quantity over time. Electrons are among the particles that make up atoms; they circle around the atom's nucleus. The other particles in atoms are protons (A), which are positively charged; and neutrons (C), which have no charge. Protons and neutrons are in the atom's nucleus. Amperes (D), or "amps" for short, are the standard metric units for measuring electrical current.

30. C: Light therapy is a beauty treatment that uses red and/or blue LED (light-emitting diode, a semiconductor source of light) to reduce hyperpigmentation (A) such as age spots, sun damage, freckles; darkened skin from metabolic or circulatory inadequacies; signs of aging like wrinkles and loose skin (B), as well as enlarged pores; reducing inflammation and scarring; and treating acne by killing bacteria (D). It can stimulate blood circulation, accelerate cellular growth, stimulate collagen production, and improve the tightness and elasticity of the skin.

Hair Care and Services

31. D: The medulla is the innermost layer of a hair shaft. The cortex is the middle layer of the hair shaft's structure. The cuticle is the outermost layer of the hair fiber or shaft.

32. C: The cells of the outermost, or Henle, layer of the hair's inner root sheath (IRS) keratinize first. The cells of the innermost layer of the IRS, or IRS cuticle, and the cells of the hair shaft's cuticle, are integrated; these cells keratinize together second. Third and last, the cells of the middle or Huxley layer of the IRS keratinize. The IRS cuticle's cells interlock with the hair shaft cuticle's cells. Being attached, these cells ascend as one in the follicular canal. The three layers of cells of the IRS keratinize at a low point in the hair follicle, and can be identified separately just above the dermal papilla; higher, up to the middle (isthmus) of the hair follicle, they work as a single entity to coat and support the hair shaft.

33. B: The hair's porosity is its ability to retain or hold moisture. However, hair that is extremely porous will both absorb more moisture and lose moisture more easily. Hair that is very fine, damaged, or both is more porous. Extremely porous hair will soak up moisture more readily, but not hold it (A). Very porous hair is absorbent; it does not repel moisture, but neither does it retain or hold it (C). Very porous hair does not repel moisture but absorbs it, but also loses it (D) easily.

34. A: The anagen phase is the stage when new hairs are actively growing. This stage can last from three to 10 years, and at any time 90 percent of the hairs on the head are in the anagen phase. The catagen phase (B) is a transitional period when the hair follicle contracts and separates from the dermal papilla which was feeding it, and the hair bulb is eliminated. This phase typically lasts one or two weeks and involves less than one percent of the hairs on the head at any time. Fully grown hairs are shed either during the telogen or resting phase (C), or following it during the next anagen phase when newly growing hairs push the old ones out of the follicle. This third phase typically lasts three to six months and involves 10 percent of the hairs on the head at any one time. Because choice (A) both lasts the longest and involves the most hairs at a time, choice (D) is incorrect.

35. B: Shampoo formulas are more alkaline than the hair and skin, allowing them to clean away dirt, oil, and styling products. After using one shampoo for a long time, the hair can develop a pH closer to the shampoo's alkalinity, and/or reach saturation levels with a certain shampoo's ingredients. This causes the hair to respond less to that shampoo and show fewer of its previous benefits. Switching to a different shampoo will solve this. Because the hair can also eventually develop a tolerance to the new shampoo, one can then switch back to the first shampoo. Therefore, changing shampoos permanently (A) will not work. Using the same shampoo more or less often (C) will not solve the hair's tolerance as a different shampoo will. As explained, hair can develop a tolerance to the same shampoo over time; this tolerance is NOT a myth (D).

36. C: Some volume at the top of the head will make a round head/face look longer and more oval. Hair that is sleek along the sides of the face, and longer than chin-length, will also minimize facial roundness. "Big" hairstyles with a lot of volume do not make a round face look smaller by contrast (A), they make the head and face look bigger, as does short, curly hair (B). Conversely, very short, "gamine" hairstyles also make the head and face look bigger (D) and will not flatter a "moon face." Balance is a key element in hairstyles. A narrower, longer style will best balance a face that is wider and shorter than the ideal oval shape.

37. D: Hot rollers are used to set the hair in thermal styling (A). Non-heated rollers are used to set the hair in wet-set styling (B). Perm rods are the types of rollers used in permanent styling (C) with a chemical permanent solution. Therefore, different kinds of rollers are used in all these types of styling.

38. C: Stylists are most likely to cornrow or tightly braid the client's own hair in order to sew hair extensions onto the original rows of hair. After sewing on extensions, the stylist pulls some of the client's own hair over the braided and sewn places. Extensions that clip into the natural hair (A) typically do not require braiding. When extensions are glued into the hair (B), the stylist uses a drop of special glue and then bonds the natural and extension hairs together using a special iron that activates the glue. Cornrowing is usually not done before gluing either. Therefore, option (C) is most likely and option (D) is incorrect.

39. B: When people grow old (but not bald), their hair can grow as slowly as one-tenth of an inch per month. One inch a month (A) and eight-tenths of an inch per month (D) are actually faster than normal growth rates for hair on a younger person. A half-inch per month (B) is the normal growth rate of most average, non-elderly people's hair.

40. A: The average person with a healthy scalp and a full head of hair has around 100,000 hairs on his or her head. Ten thousand (B) is only one-tenth of the normal approximate number of hairs. One million (C) is 10 times the normal approximate number. Twenty thousand (D) is one-fifth of the normal approximate number of hairs.

41. B: A healthy person who is not balding will normally lose about 100 hairs every day. These old hairs fall out as the growth of new hairs pushes them out from the roots. Healthy people typically lose more hairs daily than 50 (A) or 25 (C), but only half as many as 200 (D).

42. C: Dandruff and dry scalp both produce flakes of dead skin that fall from the scalp. However, while dry scalp can cause itching, dandruff causes even more itching, plus irritation, redness, and larger skin flakes that are also often greasy/oily and have an odor, rather than vice versa (A). Infection is believed to be the cause of dandruff rather than of dry scalp (B). Hence, though people often confuse them, dandruff and dry scalp are not the same (D).

43. D: Various brands of over-the-counter (OTC) shampoos and conditioners contain medications to treat mild dandruff. Antiseptic scalp lotions also help. Serious dandruff can require a doctor visit. Using scalp steamers or wrapping the head in warm, moist towels (A) is a common treatment for dry scalp, which is not the same condition as dandruff. Deep conditioning scalp treatments (B), scalp massage, and salon treatments using high-frequency direct current (D.C.) (C) are also common treatments for dry scalp rather than for dandruff.

44. C: Both oily scalp (A) and dry scalp (B) benefit from thoroughly brushing the hair and massaging the scalp. Brushing redistributes scalp oil along the length of the hair shaft, reducing the amount of oil at the scalp and roots and nourishing and protecting the rest of the hair. Scalp massage increases blood circulation to the scalp and regulates the production of sebum (oil) for oily scalp. Brushing removes dead skin flakes; massage stimulates blood circulation to the scalp, which also helps dry scalp. Thus, brushing and massaging help both conditions, so neither (D) is incorrect.

45. B: Benzoyl peroxide is a popular treatment for acne on facial and body skin, but it should be avoided for scalp acne because it can bleach the hair color (natural and/or dyed color). The same is true for other products containing peroxide ingredients. Salicylic acid (A) is another popular acne

treatment and can be safely used on the scalp without affecting hair color. It is as common for oily scalp conditions and scalp acne to occur together as it is for oily skin and acne to coexist in other places. For people with scalp acne and oily scalps, oily scalp shampoo (C) is helpful, followed with applying an astringent lotion (D) or other acne treatment using cotton pads or cotton balls. It is important to rinse away acne cleansers completely and to apply acne cleansers and treatments only to affected scalp areas because if these products get on the surrounding hair, they will strip it and dry it out too much.

46. A: While some stylists or salons opt for more expensive hair capes with the expectation that they will last longer (B), experts advise that cheaper capes can last as long as, or longer than, more expensive ones if the salon or stylist buy(s) several and rotate(s) their use. Hair capes made for shampooing and chemical treatments are heavier than styling capes, but are usually the least expensive. Their weight can make them uncomfortable for clients having several services in a row to wear them for a long time. Hair capes made for styling are cooler and lighter in weight than capes for shampooing and chemicals, but they offer much less protection against liquids dripping through them onto the client's clothes (D).

47. B: When cutting hair, tightly woven synthetic fabrics that are slippery are best because the cut hairs slide off of them. Rough-textured fabrics (A) are better for services involving liquids because they absorb moisture; however, when cutting hair, the hair sticks to these fabrics and gets on the client's neck and under the clothing when the cape is removed. Plastic capes (C) are meant for chemical processes and shampooing because they are waterproof and prevent bleaching and staining of client clothing. They can make clients uncomfortably hot if used for haircutting. They are also designed for use with towels inside and outside the cape around the client's neck, so they tend to have less secure closures than styling capes, which are made for haircutting. Fabric capes should not be avoided (D): it is easier to mend split seams or tears in them, whereas torn plastic capes must be replaced.

48. C: Shampoo attendants generally find that they get better tips when they massage the client's hair during shampooing because most clients enjoy it. Scalp massage is also beneficial for stimulating blood circulation to the hair follicles, not inhibiting it (A); and for assuring a plentiful supply of nutrients and oils to the hair shafts, not limiting it (B). Experts caution stylists not to massage using larger finger motions (D), especially with kinky or very curly hair, because it can cause matting and/or tangling.

49. D: Cleansing agents in shampoos (and some other cleansing products, like laundry detergents) are called surfactants. The molecule of a surfactant has a "head" that is hydrophilic (B), meaning that it attracts water, and a "tail" that is lipophilic (C), meaning that it attracts fats/oils. The dual water- and oil-attracting actions of the surfactant cause opposing "push-pull" forces on the oil in the hair, which also contains dirt and dead skin (and often styling products too). This effect lifts the oil, dirt, and skin off the hair shaft. When rinsing the shampoo out with water, the hydrophilic "heads" of the surfactants in the shampoo are drawn away from the hair by the water. Choices (B) and (C) are parts of (D). Because option (D) is correct, option (A) is incorrect.

50. C: The best rule for everybody is to shampoo their hair only when it is dirty or oily. Many people shampoo every day (A), but experts say this is too often. Daily shampooing, especially if not followed by conditioning, can dry the hair out; and daily shampooing and conditioning can make fine, limp hair worse. Individual needs vary, so some people will get the best results from shampooing twice a week (B) while others may only shampoo once a week (D). The only thing experts recommend doing every day to clean hair if needed is using a rinse-out conditioner, but not

- 24 -

shampoo. They say individuals should start by shampooing every other day, and then add one more day at a time between washing, until they arrive at the shampooing schedule that is right for them.

51. B: Undercutting, also called inverse layering, involves cutting the inner layers of the hair ends shorter, removing much of the bulk underneath so the outer layers can curve under more easily. This is usually aided after cutting by styling. Overcutting (A) would be the opposite of undercutting. The layering is done to the inner layers, not the outer (C) ones. The top layers are longer, not shorter (D) than the bottom layers.

52. A: To determine the growth pattern of hair, it is best to allow it to air-dry after washing. Letting it dry naturally preserves the appearance of how it grows out of the scalp. Blow-drying the hair (B) redirects the hair's movement, making it harder to see its natural direction. While it is possible to look at one's own hair at the crown and/or back using mirrors (C), this is not the easiest way. Some people may ask a friend to help, but unless the friend is a hairstylist or knowledgeable about hair, an experienced hairstylist (D) is the best choice to look at the hair and tell the client how it grows in these areas.

53. B: Many people actually have such unusual hair growth patterns. Some have straight and curly hairs growing in a mixed pattern. Others have mainly straight or mainly curly hair with one area growing differently. Therefore, that this never happens (C) is not true. In some cases, environmental stress can cause differences; for example, if someone always sleeps on one side, but also sleeps restlessly, the hair on the side that is always rubbing against the pillow may look frizzy while the other side appears smooth. However, environmental stress is not the only cause (A). The causes may be environmental or genetic, but it is not true that such mixed growth patterns are only due to a rare genetic defect (D).

54. C: Naturally blond hair is the densest: it tends to have about 27-30 percent more hairs per square inch than naturally black (B) or brown (D) hair has. Naturally red (A) hair is the least dense, averaging only about 70-72 percent of the number of hairs per square inch that dark hair colors have.

55. D: To achieve balance for an overweight person, the hairstyle should have more vertical than horizontal volume to make the face look more oval and the head and body longer. Many overweight people, especially those with more upper-body weight or "apple" shapes, look as though their heads are small in proportion to their bodies, and short hairstyles (A) only make this worse. However, overly "big" hairdos (B) are also unflattering by adding to the bulk of the upper body. Adding horizontal volume (C) makes the face look wider.

56. C: Hairstylists with a lot of experience in cutting with clippers can taper a man's hair simply by using the clippers-over-comb method, but this is not for the inexperienced (A). For those with less experience, or even those with more experience who want to make the haircut the safest, many clippers come with attachments for tapering short hair around the ears. Such attachments have angled combs with teeth of graduated lengths, rather than teeth of all one uniform length (B). With these attachments, the shortest comb length is always for the hair's bottom edge, not the top (D).

57. B: Of the choices given, the most realistic advice to a client wanting a style at odds with his/her hair type is that fine, thin hair can be made to look fuller through various styling products and methods, but not extremely "big" with its natural texture and density. Using choice (A) would make the hair look somewhat "bigger," but the client with unrealistic expectations will likely be dissatisfied; plus, trying to maintain the style at home would involve excessive work and hair

damage. It is more realistic to make the hair look somewhat fuller than deny the possibility completely and advise a style so opposite as a very short cut (C). While a wig is a good possibility for truly "big" hair, the stylist should only suggest this; it is not as realistic to recommend it as the only option (D) because the client may not want to wear a wig.

58. A: The common reference for haircutting angles is in relation to the floor. For instance, if the stylist cuts the hair at a 45-degree angle, this means s/he holds the scissors at an angle of 45 degrees from the floor; i.e., halfway between 90 degrees or vertical/perpendicular to the floor and zero degrees or horizontal/parallel with the floor. Haircutting angles do not refer to their relationship to the hairs (B), the hand (C) holding the scissors, or the face (D) of the client whose hair is being cut.

59. B: The parietal ridges are directly below the top of the head, where the top meets the sides of the head. The occipital bone (A) is lower down, where the skull meets the neck at the back of the head and neck. The crown of the head (C) is behind the top of the head and the parietal ridges, not directly beneath the top, and it extends both above and below the parietal ridges between the top of the head and the occipital bone. The temples (D) are below the fronts of the parietal ridges.

60. C: The description is of one kind of cross-checking, done early in the haircut while establishing lengths for front, side, and back hair to make sure the two side lengths match. Over-direction (A) is elevating or lifting hair sections past the 90-degree mark, horizontally straight-out-from-the-head position, against the direction it naturally falls, when cutting. Hair sectioning (B) is parting the hair into sections to be cut separately. (Some sections are also wound up and clipped on top of the head to get them out of the way of sections to be cut first.) Back-combing (D) the hair is a synonym for teasing the hair. Although another method of cross-checking, done later when all hair sections have been cut to check layering, involves combing sections against the cutting direction to reveal any missed hairs, this is not called "back-combing," but simply "cross-checking."

61. D: The standard sections for haircutting are seven: the top of the head, the left side, the right side, the left crown, the right crown, the left nape, and the right nape. The other choices are not enough to include all of these head areas for sectioning the hair before cutting it.

62. C: In haircutting terminology, "graduated" and "layered" are more or less synonyms. However, two slight differences include: (1) that "graduated" is a term more often used in cosmetology schools and textbooks, while "layered" is a more common term in workplace cosmetology practice; and (2) that using the term "graduated" can refer to a haircut with more even layers, while "layered" can include cuts with more uneven or random layering. All graduated haircuts have layers, so option (A) is incorrect. Layered haircuts are graduated, so choice (B) is incorrect. The term "graduated" often means the layering is more even rather than "layered," so option (D) is incorrect.

63. B: Braiding has many advantages for children's hair as well as being a stylish option for adults' hair. Although there are some more elaborate braiding styles, braids are not always complicated or time-consuming to fashion (A). The simplest braids can be formed quite quickly with minimal practice, an advantage taken by many busy parents. Another advantage of braiding children's hair is that the braids will keep their shape longer than other hairstyles (C), requiring less maintenance. An additional advantage of braiding children's hair is that the braids will prevent their hair from tangling, snarling, or matting (D) during an active day, making it easier to comb out after the braids are undone.

64. A: When pulled out of a wig and burnt, natural (real) hair will burn slowly with a distinctive "burnt hair" smell. Synthetic hair does NOT give off an odor when burnt (B). Depending on its composition, synthetic hair will melt (C) and/or ball up (D) when burnt, or will burn out more quickly (D) than natural hair. However, real hair burns slower, not faster than synthetic hair (C), and real hair will not ball up (D) the way some synthetic hair will when burnt.

65. B: A skin patch test should always be made on a client before any and all chemical services to make sure the client's skin does not have allergies or sensitivities to any of the ingredients. Skin patch tests should be made of all ingredients in hair color, permanent waving solutions, straightening (A) formulas, relaxers, and more. Developers used in coloring hair are bleaching agents that can irritate the skin, and must be patch-tested on the skin as well as the hair coloring formulas (C). Any skin patch test should be done 24-48 hours before any planned chemical service, not 8-12 (D) to allow enough time for a reaction to be observed (e.g., redness, itchiness, swelling). The chemical service planned should NOT be done if any skin reaction occurs. Even a reaction that seems minuscule can be drastically magnified when the amount and time of exposure are increased as much as most chemical services involve.

66. C: Cold waves, so-called because they need no added heat to process quickly, are alkaline and hence have the highest pH, usually from 9.0 to 9.6. They give strong curling but can damage delicate hair and have a strong ammonia smell. Acid waves (A) are less alkaline, with a pH of 4.5 to 7.0. They take longer to process, require added heat, produce less firm curling, and are gentler on delicate, damaged, and porous hair. "Acid-balanced" (B) wave solutions have a pH of 7.8 to 8.2, so they are not alkaline but not truly acidic either. They process faster, require no additional heat, and make firmer curls than true acid waves while still being gentler than alkaline solutions on damaged and porous hair. Wave solutions based on sulfites (D), bisulfites, and sulfates instead of ammonium thioglycolate/thiol compounds have the lowest pH and are gentle on fine and/or damaged hair. While they not giving firm curls, they are good for loose curls, gentle waves, or body waves.

67. D: Green will cancel out red. According to the laws of color, colors that are the opposite of each other, and are seen opposite/across from each other on the color wheel, are called complimentary colors. The term complimentary relates to how these colors go together well in color schemes when kept distinct. When mixed in equal parts, they produce brown or gray. In coloring hair, too much of one color can be neutralized or balanced out by its compliment. Blue (A) cancels out orange. Yellow (B) cancels out violet, and conversely, violet (C) cancels out yellow. Green cancels out red and vice versa.

68. D: Temporary hair color rinses are called temporary because they typically last only until the next shampoo, which will wash the color out of the hair. Semi-permanent and demi-permanent hair colors typically last for about eight to 12 shampoos (A). By contrast, temporary color does not last through even two or three shampoos (B) or four to six shampoos (C), but is shampooed out because it rests on the outside of the cuticle without penetrating into it.

69. C: Only permanent hair color can lighten the hair's natural color. Semi-permanent color (A) deposits color into the hair's cuticle but does not lighten the original hair color. Demi-permanent color (B) deposits color into the hair's cuticle and also deeper into its cortex, but will not lighten the original hair color either. Permanent hair color contains hydrogen peroxide developer to let the color molecules penetrate into the hair's cortex; when it contains a stronger developer, this will also lighten the original hair color. Because only option (C) is correct, option (D) is incorrect. For coloring without lightening, the colorist typically uses a developer with 10-volume peroxide; to lighten hair one or two levels, 20-volume peroxide; and 30- or 40-volume peroxide to lighten more

than two levels. (For drastic lightening, as with changing black hair to platinum blonde, an extra step is needed to strip the hair of all color with even stronger peroxide bleach before adding the new color in the next step.)

70. B: The best approach would be to select some strands of the hair that is now colored the lighter golden brown and protect these with foils, and then color the rest of the hair darker like the client's original color (without the gray). This will achieve the effect the client originally wanted. Bleaching to create highlights (A) is unnecessary because all of her hair is already the color of the highlights she wanted. She does not have to do without highlights (C); the lighter color she ended up with is the color of the highlights she wanted. All she needs is for the rest of her hair to be darker again. Stripping the hair and starting over (D) is completely unnecessary in this scenario and would needlessly damage the hair. Color correction is much less drastic when all that is needed is to make most of the hair a couple of shades darker.

Skin Care and Services

71. A: The dermis is the middle layer of the skin, made of connective tissue whose main substance is collagen. The epidermis (B) is the outer layer of the skin, made of keratinized, stratified squamous epithelium. The dermis gradually changes into the hypodermis (C), the innermost layer of the skin which contains adipose (fatty) tissue. The stratum corneum (D) is one layer within four layers (strata) of the epidermis.

72. C: The sebaceous glands are the oil glands associated with the hair follicles and hair shafts. Eccrine (A) and apocrine (B) glands are the two types of sweat glands in the skin. Tubular glands (D) are a simple type of gland; both types of sweat glands are simple tubular glands. The sebaceous glands are known as holocrine glands and differ from all the other kinds of glands.

73. B: Melanin is the pigment produced by melanocytes in the skin. It gives the epidermis (outer layer of skin) a yellowish or brownish color. The amount of melanin affects the color of skin on different parts of the body. The dermis (A), or middle layer of skin, varies in thickness, which also affects the color of skin on different parts of the body. Collagen (C), a connective tissue, reflects white light and gives lighter skin its "white" color. The hemoglobin (D) in the red blood cells contributes the pink color to areas of skin without pigment.

74. A: Melanoma is less common than the other types of skin cancer, but is the most dangerous. It is estimated to cause around 75 percent of all deaths related to skin cancer. Basal cell carcinoma (A) is the most common skin cancer, making up around 80 percent of all skin cancer cases. It grows slowly and seldom spreads from its original site to other areas. Squamous cell carcinoma (C) is more aggressive than basal cell carcinoma, but not as serious as melanoma. Because choice (A) has the combination of least common and most dangerous, choice (D) is incorrect.

75. B: Rosacea is a skin condition that causes redness and broken capillaries. If a cosmetologist discovers signs of rosacea during a skin analysis, s/he will use little or no steam, and little or no pressure if doing any extractions, to avoid damaging the skin further. Steam can be beneficial for acne (A) by opening up clogged pores. Steam and pressure can both help in extracting blackheads (C) and/or whiteheads (D).

76. D: To give a facial treatment, the cosmetologist should first use a hairband (C) to pull all of the client's hair away from the face, to keep facial products from getting into the hair, and also to keep

the hair off the face. Then s/he should wrap a professional service towel (B) around the client's neck to keep products from dripping onto the neck. Then s/he should drape a cape (A) over the client to protect the client's clothing.

77. C: Tweezers with slanted tips are recommended for general grooming and shaping of the eyebrows. Tweezers with pointed tips (A) are recommended for plucking out ingrown hairs, stubby hairs, and fine hairs because they have the finest tips. Tweezers with square tips (B) are best for tweezing larger areas because they have the biggest gripping surfaces. (Very large areas should not be tweezed as this can cause scars and/or ingrown hairs.) Because each kind of tip is best for a different use, option (D) is incorrect.

78. B: Threading is a method of hair removal that dates back to ancient times, so it is not new (A). Threading is typically less painful than waxing, although it does pull out the hairs (C) from their follicles the same as waxing does. Threading, like waxing, does last longer than shaving or depilatories; however, it is still a temporary method of removing hair rather than a permanent one (D).

79. A: Sugaring is a process similar to waxing in that a substance is heated, applied to the skin, and then ripped away to pull out the hair. However, unlike wax, sugaring uses a solution of sugar, lemon juice, and water. These natural ingredients make sugaring gentler than other methods that use various chemicals, as sugaring uses no chemical ingredients (C). Sugaring, like threading, is a hair removal method with ancient origins rather than a recent innovation (B). Also like threading, sugaring is very popular in Eastern and Middle Eastern cultures rather than being limited to Western culture (D). In fact, Western culture acquired the threading and sugaring methods from Eastern cultures.

80. D: Between one client and the next, cosmetology operators must always clean their instruments using soap and water (A), and then immerse them completely in a disinfectant that is registered with the EPA (Environmental Protection Agency) and kills bacteria (B), fungi, and viruses (C). Bacterial infections, fungal infections, and viruses including Hepatitis B and HIV can be spread to clients if instruments are not properly cleaned and disinfected.

81. A: Electric facials stimulate the facial and neck muscles, which plumps them up and activates them. Dermatologists and facialists use electric treatments as a complement to Botox injections by giving them a few weeks after the Botox. They do not remove fat or slim the face (B); they make facial contours rounder. They are also used to lift facial areas by shortening muscles, and to smooth furrows by stretching muscles. They do not deliver a current equal to a light bulb's (C): a typical light bulb uses less than one ampere of current, whereas electric facials deliver only one one-millionth of an ampere. This amount is called a low level of microcurrent. Botox and similar neurotoxins stop wrinkles temporarily via muscle paralysis, not electric facials (D).

82. B: It is not true that no topical cream works as a filler (A) like injections do. There are some that use ingredients similar to those in injections (e.g., Metahylate Complex) and instantly plump up the skin, filling in wrinkles and other flaws. Additionally, such topical preparations can stimulate regeneration of the skin cells and treat wrinkles in the long term, which are benefits that injected fillers do not give (C). Only some topical dermal filler products are effective, however; not all brands are the same (D). One must research different brands before use because most are expensive and some have no more effect than ordinary wrinkle creams. Those that are effective are not yet widely used (D).

83. C: Adding black to a true color or hue will darken it, producing a shade of that color. A tint (A) of a color is produced by adding white to make it lighter. A tone (B) of a color is produced by adding gray to it, making it more muted. Value (D) refers to how light or dark a color is between black and white; for example, pink, a tint of red, has a lighter value while maroon, a shade of red, has a darker value.

84. D: Everyday makeup is more likely to be basic makeup and less likely to be specialty makeup than the other choices. Theatrical makeup that actors wear onstage in plays (A), monster/creature makeup applied for movies or TV shows (B), and makeup worn as part of a Halloween costume (C) are all examples of specialty makeups.

85. C: The eyes are very delicate, so even a seemingly minor irritation to the eye can cause damage and even blindness. Not only are many people allergic to the adhesives (A) used to affix eyelashes, they can also be allergic to the material used in the lashes themselves (B). Cosmetologists can avoid being held liable (D) for eye damage and/or allergy symptoms by requiring a preliminary patch test; moreover, they can avoid causing harm, discomfort, or inconvenience to clients by doing so.

Nail Care and Services

86. D: Keratin is a fibrous, structural protein that comprises the fingernails and toenails. It is also the main substance of the outer layer of human skin, and the chief structural protein of human hair. The perionychium (A) is the skin covering the side edges of the nail. This is where hangnails occur. The hyponychium (B) is a waterproof barrier and the junction where the fingertip or toe joins with the free edge of the nail. The eponychium (C), also called the cuticle, is also a waterproof barrier and connects the finger or toe skin to the nail plate where it grows out of the finger or toe.

87. C: Nail pitting (A), or little pits or indentations in the nails, can be secondary to the skin condition psoriasis. (It can also be caused by Reiter syndrome, a reactive arthritis secondary to bacterial infection; other connective tissue disorders; and alopecia areata, an autoimmune disease causing local hair loss.) Psoriasis can also cause separation (B) of the nails from the nail beds. (Nail injuries, infections, thyroid disease, and reactions to nail hardeners or adhesives can also cause the nails to separate.) Spoon nails (D), i.e., nails that are soft and indented or depressed, looking "scooped out" like the bowls of spoons, can be secondary to iron deficiency anemia, hemochromatosis, heart disease, or hypothyroidism, but not psoriasis.

88. B: The average length of time that human fingernails take for complete regrowth is three to six months, while human toenails take an average time of 12-18 months. These rates vary somewhat around the averages according to factors including heredity, age, gender, diet, exercise, and the season of the year.

89. A: Terry's nails can sometimes be caused simply by aging. However, this condition can also be a sign of something more serious, including liver disease (B), congestive heart failure (C), or diabetes (D). Therefore, Terry's nails can be secondary to any and all of these conditions.

90. B: Yellow nail syndrome is frequently associated with chronic bronchitis or other respiratory diseases. Although yellow nail syndrome shares symptoms of nail thickening and yellowing in common with nail fungus, it is NOT caused by fungus and is NOT a name for nail fungus (A). Another condition that yellow nail syndrome CAN be associated with is lymphedema (C), which is a

swelling caused by fluid buildup in the hands. Yellow nail syndrome CAN cause nails to separate from the nail bed and CAN also cause loss of the cuticle(s) (D).

91. C: Certain kinds of metal nail files can be disinfected using salon disinfectant approved by and registered with the EPA to kill bacteria, fungi, and viruses. Nail files that can be fully disinfected do not have to be thrown away after use on a client. However, cotton balls and/or pads (A) cannot be disinfected and must be thrown out immediately after use. Emery boards (B) also cannot be disinfected and must be discarded. Therefore, choice (D) is incorrect because all of these cannot be safely saved.

92. D: The finer the grit in a nail file or abrasive, the higher its number is. For example, most over-the-counter emery boards have grits of 80 (A), which is very coarse and should not be used on real nails as it is too rough and will shred the nail's layers. An example of an implement with grit above 3600 (B) is a "three-way buffer," which is used to shine the nail surface rather than to shape the nail edges. Experts recommend using a file with a grit of at least 240 for shaping the free edges of nails; therefore, 180 is NOT a high enough number (C).

93. C: Many nail technicians would rather use a curette because, when used correctly, it scrapes the extra cuticle off the nail. A cuticle pusher (A) will not remove extra cuticle, but only push it back. For clients with excessive, dry cuticles, pushing is not sufficient and will leave a thick ridge of cuticle. Using a curette correctly eliminates the need for using cuticle nippers (B), which can more easily cut the skin accidentally. Because a curette takes the place of a cuticle pusher and cuticle nippers, all three should NOT be used together (D).

94. B: Hot oil manicures, using oil typically warmed in a hot oil machine (a heating unit designed for this purpose), are always recommended for clients with very dry nails (A), very dry skin (C), or both (B). While others may also enjoy and request them, hot oil manicures are not always recommended for all clients (D).

95. C: Experts advise that, when giving pedicures to elderly clients, pedicure tubs with massaging machines should be avoided (A) or the massage function should be turned off, and very hot water should not be used to soak the feet (B). They further recommend that, before giving a pedicure to any elderly client, it is best to consult the client's doctor (D), particularly if the client might have any debilitating and/or severe health conditions.

96. D: The regulations of the Board of Barbering and Cosmetology legally prohibit practitioners from giving massage to clients if they have any communicable disease, infection, skin inflammation, or eruption. To protect the customers and their other clients, licensed operators must refuse to perform the service under any of these conditions or similar ones.

97. C: The hand and arm massage includes gently twisting each finger in both directions and then quickly pulling each finger and thumb (A). This loosens the joints and releases muscle tension. Applying pressure between the back wrist bones (B) loosens the lymphatic veins. The base of the thumb (D) and the base of the palm are also areas that are important to give attention to during the massage.

98. B: The first step in pre-service procedures for nail care is to clean the table. Then the arm cushion should be wrapped in a sanitized towel. The disinfectant container should be filled 20 minutes before the day's first manicure, and the disinfectant changed daily or whenever debris is visible. After filling the container with disinfectant, washed and dried implements should be put

into it. Placing the manicure products on the table behind the disinfectant container is the fifth step. [Following these five, additional steps include placing abrasives (files, buffers, etc.) on the table; placing either a fingerbowl for soaking, or an electric oil heater for reconditioning manicures; placing a waste receptacle for each new manicure; and preparing a clean, organized drawer with only clean, sanitized supplies and materials, e.g., extra chamois, cotton; pumice stones or powder; flash-drying agents, etc.]

99. A: Nail tips should cover less than half of the natural nails. Covering more than half of the natural nail (B) makes the extension weaker. Nail tips add length and shape to natural or artificial nails, but they do not add durability or strength (C). Only the complete overlays of acrylic, gel, or fiberglass nails, applied after the nail tips, will provide durability and strength. After application, the nail tip is visible and can be blended by filing around the seams for a more natural look; however, when filing, it is important to avoid filing on the natural nail (D), which will damage it.

100. B: Artificial nails made from gel polishes often give a more natural, glossy look than acrylic, fiberglass, or other materials. Gel nails do not cure with exposure to the air like acrylic nails, but must be hardened with UV light; however, they take less time, not more, to cure than acrylic (A). While gel nails frequently must be filed off, it is not true that they can never be soaked off like acrylic nails (C): there are some kinds of gel nails that can be soaked off without filing or damaging the nail beds. Gel nails cost more than acrylic nails, but they tend not to last as long as acrylic (D). (Gel is also considered safer and more environmentally friendly because it does not have the fumes of acrylic.)

Practice Test #2

Practice Questions

Scientific Concepts

1. To kill all microbes and spores, instruments must be…
   a. Sterilized.
   b. Sanitized.
   c. Disinfected.
   d. None of the above

2. After using a foot spa basin, the cosmetologist should clean and then disinfect its surfaces with a hospital disinfectant that is registered with which of the following agencies?
   a. The FDA
   b. The EPA
   c. The CDC
   d. The OSHA

3. Which of these are the main storage units in the human body's cells?
   a. Mitochondria
   b. Lysosomes
   c. Vacuoles
   d. Nuclei

4. In human cells, _____ constitutes genetic material and _____ makes and transports copies of it.
   a. Plasma; cytoplasm
   b. Cytoplasm; plasma
   c. RNA; DNA
   d. DNA; RNA

5. Which type of tissue in the human body serves the functions of secreting, excreting, absorbing, protecting, and perceiving sensory information?
   a. Connective
   b. Muscular
   c. Nervous
   d. Epithelial

6. Which of the following is correct regarding the blood vessels relative to the heart?
   a. Blood is pumped away from and back to the heart via arteries and is contained in the veins.
   b. Blood is pumped away from the heart through veins and back to the heart through arteries.
   c. Blood is pumped away from the heart through arteries and back to the heart through veins.
   d. Blood is pumped both away from and back to the heart through either the arteries or veins.

7. Of the following ways in which human lungs protect themselves, which one does so by filtering?
   a. The mucus
   b. The nose
   c. The cilia
   d. The cough

8. The melanocytes, cells that make the pigment that colors a person's skin, are found in which skin layer?
   a. In the epidermis
   b. In the subcutis
   c. In the dermis
   d. All of the above

9. Which of the following facial bones is a single bone rather than a pair of bones?
   a. The mandible
   b. The lacrimal
   c. The maxilla
   d. The nasal

10. Of the following bones, which is/are closely related to the skull but not located within the skull?
    a. The frontal bone
    b. The hyoid bone
    c. The atlas bone
    d. The ossicles

11. Which of the shoulder bones includes the acromion, coracoid process, and spine?
    a. The clavicle
    b. The humerus
    c. The scapula
    d. The radius

12. The bones found in the lower arm are the...
    a. Humerus and ulna.
    b. Carpal and metacarpal.
    c. Ulna and phalanges.
    d. Radius and ulna.

13. What is the name of the bones found in the ankle?
    a. Metatarsals
    b. Calcaneus
    c. The tarsals
    d. Phalanges

14. Of the muscles involved in chewing, which one opens the jaw?
    a. The medial pterygoid
    b. The lateral pterygoid
    c. The masseter muscle
    d. The temporalis muscle

15. Which of the following is true about the tongue?
    a. It is a muscle itself and also contains muscles.
    b. It is not a muscle itself but contains muscles.
    c. It is a muscle itself but contains no muscles.
    d. It is neither a muscle nor contains muscles.

16. Which kind of eye movement keeps people from having double vision?
    a. Tremor
    b. Vergence
    c. Drift
    d. Flick

17. Which nose muscle(s) is/are responsible for opening and flaring the nostrils?
    a. The Pyramidalis nasi
    b. The Depressor septi
    c. The Dilatator narises
    d. The Compressor naris

18. The human hand has over __ different muscles.
    a. 30
    b. 40
    c. 50
    d. 60

19. Writing, picking up objects, building, making things, and other activities depending on manual dexterity are enabled by...
    a. Disks in the wrists.
    b. The thenar muscles.
    c. Opposable thumbs.
    d. Hypothenar muscles.

20. Muscles that move the legs outward are called _____, while muscles that move the legs inward are called _____.
    a. Adductors; abductors
    b. Abductors; adductors
    c. Flexors; extensors
    d. Extensors; flexors

21. The human shoulder joint has more _____ than _____.
    a. Mobility; stability
    b. Stability; mobility
    c. Strength; mobility
    d. Stability; strength

22. In the human cardiovascular system, the veins in the stomach and intestines carry blood to the...
    a. Heart.
    b. Liver.
    c. Kidneys.
    d. Lungs.

23. Which gland in the endocrine system has dual functions as both an endocrine and exocrine gland?
   a. The pituitary
   b. The thyroid
   c. The pancreas
   d. The adrenals

24. Which of the following body parts that cosmetologists work with are included in the integumentary system?
   a. Hair
   b. Skin
   c. Nails
   d. All of the above

25. Urine is liquid waste filtered out of the blood. Which of the following gives the correct order, from first to last, of urine's journey through the body and out of it?
   a. Urethra, kidneys, bladder, ureters
   b. Ureters, urethra, bladder, kidneys
   c. Kidneys, ureters, bladder, urethra
   d. Ureters, urethra, kidneys, bladder

26. Of the four states of matter, which one is the state found in lightning, stars, and inside of neon signs and fluorescent lights?
   a. Solids
   b. Plasma
   c. Liquids
   d. Gases

27. Chemically, excessive amounts of nutrients like _____ can build up to unsafe levels in the blood while excessive amounts of nutrients like _____ can be excreted out of the body.
   a. Fat-soluble vitamins; water-soluble vitamins
   b. Water-soluble vitamins; fat-soluble vitamins
   c. Water-soluble vitamins; dietary minerals
   d. Fat-soluble vitamins; trace elements

28. Which statement correctly reflects differences between compounds and mixtures?
   a. Mixtures can only be separated chemically; compounds can be separated mechanically.
   b. Compounds can only be separated chemically; mixtures can be separated mechanically.
   c. Mixtures can only be created chemically, while compounds can be created mechanically.
   d. Compound properties are more like their parts' properties than mixture properties are.

29. Which of the following electrotherapy beauty treatments is known as a nonsurgical facelift?
   a. Galvanic treatment
   b. High-frequency treatment
   c. NMES or Faradic treatment
   d. MENS or micro-current treatment

30. Which of the following is most accurate about the EPA's Design for the Environment program?
    a. It labels various products to show their safety rather than effectiveness.
    b. It labels various products to show their safety only for health of humans.
    c. It labels various products to show their safety for the environment only.
    d. It labels various products to show their environmental and health safety.

Hair Care and Services

31. The part of a hair under the skin is the ___, whose base is the ___, which is encased in a pocket in the skin called the ___, which is nourished by a small, conical bump at its bottom called the ___.
    a. Bulb; root; dermal papilla; follicle
    b. Follicle; dermal papilla; root; bulb
    c. Root; bulb; follicle; dermal papilla
    d. Dermal papilla; root; bulb; follicle

32. If a person's hair is straight, his/her hair follicles are ___; if someone's hair is wavy or curly, the hair follicles are ___.
    a. Oval; round
    b. Round; oval
    c. Large; small
    d. Small; large

33. Hair with higher water intake has more _____, and has more of this when wet, even if damaged.
    a. Elasticity
    b. Porosity
    c. Texture
    d. Density

34. Which of the following diseases or disorders is most likely to cause abnormal hair breakage?
    a. Loose Anagen Syndrome
    b. Trichorrhexis Nodosa
    c. Seborrheic Dermatitis
    d. Folliculitis

35. A client with straight, fine, soft hair wants a short and layered "pixie" cut. She also wants the different layers to look very distinct. Which is the most accurate statement about this hair type and hairstyle?
    a. This is not the best cut for her hair type; the client would be better off with a longer blunt cut.
    b. This client should not have a short cut because her fine hair will make her head look smaller.
    c. This is a good style for the hair type, but layers will not be too visible without highlighting or styling.
    d. This is the best style for this client because the layering will stand out the most with her hair type.

36. Which of the following is most true about safely giving razor haircuts?
    a. When stylists take a licensing test, they must use razors with and without guards.
    b. Given the right tools, a hairstylist does not need experience to do good razor cuts.
    c. Hairstylists with years of experience using razors never cut using the blade guards.
    d. Most state licensing agencies require blade guards on razors during licensure tests.

37. When comparing synthetic hair wigs to natural hair wigs, which is true about advantages and disadvantages?
    a. Synthetic hair wigs last longer and withstand heat.
    b. Natural hair wigs are less expensive than synthetic.
    c. Synthetic hair wigs need no restyling after washing.
    d. Natural hair wigs are harder to color than synthetic.

38. About how fast does the average hair grow on a healthy, non-elderly person?
    a. About one inch per month
    b About a half-inch per month
    c. About a quarter-inch per month
    d. About two inches per month

39. Under normal conditions, how long will each hair on the head of a healthy person last?
    a. From one to six years
    b. From two to four years
    c. From three to five years
    d. From six months to one year

40. Which of the following most accurately identifies the reason for baldness?
    a. All the person's hair has fallen out.
    b. New hairs are no longer produced.
    c. Old hairs fall out faster than usual.
    d. New hairs fall faster than is typical.

41. Which of the following is true about the rate of hair growth on different parts of the head?
    a. Hair grows faster in the bangs than other head areas.
    b. Hair grows the fastest on the crown part of the head.
    c. Hair grows at around the same rate all over the head.
    d. Hair grows at the fastest rate at the nape of the neck.

42. Which of the following scalp conditions can lead to hair loss if not treated?
    a. Dry scalp
    b. Both
    c. Neither
    d. Dandruff

43. What is the best way for someone with long hair to treat an oily scalp?
    a. Shampoo and condition from the scalp to the ends every day
    b. Apply astringents/oil-removing tonics from scalp to ends daily
    c. Work shampoo into the scalp only and moisturize only the ends
    d. Either shampoo daily without conditioner, or less often with it

44. After shampooing, conditioning, and thoroughly rinsing, how does a final rinse with cool instead of warm water benefit the hair?
    a. It closes scalp pores, reducing oily scalp.
    b. It does both (A) and (C), but (D) is false.
    c. It closes hair cuticles, making hair shinier.
    d. It has no benefit and causes discomfort.

45. Which of the following is a scalp disease caused by a fungal infection?
    a. Tinea Capitis
    b. Trichotillomania
    c. Seborrheic Dermatitis
    d. Folliculitis

46. Which of the following is true about hair capes with snap closures versus those with Velcro closures?
    a. Snap closures last longer than Velcro closures last.
    b. Velcro lasts as long as snaps but causes hair issues.
    c. Snap closures are the best for use with neck strips.
    d. Velcro closures are best for use with salon towels.

47. What is the best way to remove a hair cape after cutting a client's hair?
    a. Remove the cape as quickly as possible to get rid of hair
    b. Undo the cape and remove the neck strip or towel first
    c. Slowly fold the back ends up and around the shoulders
    d. Lift the cape straight up vertically away from the client

48. What kind of scalp treatments can open clogged pores and increase circulation?
    a. Creams with deep conditioning
    b. Hot oil treatment preparations
    c. Treatment with heat therapies
    d. Astringents or cleansing agents

49. If a client has hair that is fine, curly, and frizzy, what is the best shampoo choice?
    a. A heavyweight conditioning shampoo designed to control frizz
    b. A shampoo for smoothing frizz and other products to add body
    c. Volumizing shampoo, then other lightweight anti-frizz products
    d. Shampoo combining ingredients for more volume and less frizz

50. When a client's hair is dry and flyaway from frequent shampooing without conditioner, but many conditioners also make it limp and greasy at the roots, what kind of conditioner is a good solution?
    a. A rinse-through conditioner
    b. A spray-on, leave-in conditioner
    c. A deep conditioning hair masque
    d. A protein pack repair conditioner

51. When creating a "pageboy" or "bob" style that curves under at the ends, which of the following is most compatible with this styling?
    a. Straight hair
    b. Very wavy hair
    c. Curly hair
    d. Humidity

52. Which of the following is true about portions of someone's hair following different directions than the rest?
    a. This can be changed easily enough by blow-dryer styling.
    b. This can only be changed by straightening hair chemically.
    c. This can occur occasionally but is a very unusual condition.
    d. This can never be observed to happen with anyone's hair.

53. If a client has two areas on the crown of the head where the hair grows in circles, which is true about how the stylist should cut it for a layered hairstyle?
    a. The stylist should cut layers very short in these spots.
    b. The stylist should hold the hair tightly while cutting it.
    c. The stylist should ensure that layers are long enough.
    d. The stylist should hold hair tighter if it is curly or wavy.

54. Which of the following combinations of hair texture and density would look the fullest?
    a. Fine texture with higher density
    b. Coarse texture with low density
    c. Finer texture with lower density
    d. Coarse texture and high density

55. If a client wants bangs with a new hairstyle and is overweight, including in the face, which is the best way to cut them?
    a. Blunt
    b. Angled
    c. (B) or (D)
    d. Side-swept

56. If a client is moving to a very hot, humid climate, has naturally wavy hair that frizzes easily, and does not want to fuss with hair much, which would be the most practical hairstyle?
    a. Long and straight
    b. Short and natural
    c. Long, loose waves
    d. Short, tight curls

57. If a person has perfectly straight hair that hangs with its ends pointing at the floor, it is said to have an elevation point of how many degrees?
    a. An elevation point of zero degrees (0°)
    b. An elevation point of 180 degrees (180°)
    c. An elevation point of 90 degrees (90°)
    d. It depends where it grows from the head

58. In terms of elevation and angle in cutting hair, which of the following is most correct?
    a. The lower the elevation and angle of cutting, the more layered the hair will be.
    b. The higher the elevation and angle of cutting, the more layered the hair will be.
    c. The lower the elevation and higher the angle, the more layered the hair will be.
    d. The higher the elevation and lower the angle, the more layered the hair will be.

59. Among texturizing techniques, which is classified as a type of smooth cutting rather than a type of internal cutting?
    a. Chipping method
    b. Weaving method
    c. Slithering and sliding
    d. Thinning scissors

60. Some hairstylists, including those with training, complain of nicking themselves when they texturize or thin hair using their haircutting shears. The most common reason for this is...
    a. Moving blades too near the hands.
    b. Moving one's thumb by itself.
    c. Moving only one of the blades.
    d. Moving both blades together.

61. In haircutting, when giving a blunt cut, how should a stylist hold the client's hair to cut it?
    a. Using full tension
    b. Use some tension
    c. Using zero tension
    d. Depends on length

62. Graduated haircuts that are longer generally feature _____ layers; graduated cuts that are shorter generally have _____ layers.
    a. Shallower; deeper
    b. Deeper; shallower
    c. More; fewer
    d. Fewer; more

63. What is most accurate about these differently named braids?
    a. Fishtail braids use a different number of hair sections.
    b. A rope braid is a braiding style distinct from any other.
    c. French braids and cornrows describe the same thing.
    d. Basic and French braids are both made the same way.

64. For someone who is bald or has very thin hair, which type of wig is a better choice?
    a. An open-cap wig
    b. The full-cap wig
    c. The cap-less wig
    d. Either is as good

65. Which of the following is true related to doing strand tests of hair before processing?
    a. It is only important to determine ideal processing time for the client.
    b. It shows if a process will damage hair so it can be repaired afterward.
    c. It is important because the hair can be totally melted in some cases.
    d. It is no more important with damaged hair or dramatic color changes.

66. Chemical hair relaxers based on hydroxides leave the hair _____, even after rinsing them out thoroughly, so a(n) _____ lotion or shampoo is used afterward.
    a. Acidic; alkalinizing
    b. Dried; moisturizing
    c. Damaged; oxidizing
    d. Alkaline; neutralizing

67. By the law of color as it relates to hair coloring pigments, if someone mixed together equal parts of all colors, what would s/he get?
    a. White
    b. Brown
    c. Black
    d. Gray

68. Which kind of hair color penetrates not only into the cuticle of the hair, but also deeper, into the hair's cortex?
    a. Semi-permanent hair color
    b. Both (C) and (D) will do this
    c. Demi-permanent hair color
    d. Permanent hair color

69. Hair colored previously with permanent color tends to be more _____ than virgin hair, so when coloring it again it is advised to _____.
    a. Porous; leave color on a shorter time
    b. Resistant; leave color on a longer time
    c. Damaged; use a hot oil treatment first
    d. Damaged; apply a protein conditioner

70. If a client dyed her hair dark brown but had porous hair and left the color on too long so it turned out black, what can a stylist do?
    a. The only immediate solution is to bleach and re-color the hair.
    b. Use peroxide with conditioner or with shampoo and low heat.
    c. Just allowing the hair to grow out is the only thing to be done.
    d. The error damaged the hair, so it cannot be processed further.

Skin Care and Services

71. Which of the following functions is NOT controlled by the skin's motor nerve endings?
    a. The flow of blood
    b. Secretion of sweat
    c. The itching function
    d. Standing up of hairs

72. Where is the epidermis of the skin the thinnest?
    a. Most of the body
    b. The soles of the feet
    c. The palms of the hands
    d. The skin over the eyelids

73. Which of the following skin conditions is known to be caused by bacterial infection?
    a. Lupus
    b. Vitiligo
    c. Cellulitis
    d. Psoriasis

74. The skin prevents the loss of body fluids, provides a protective barrier, and receives tactile sensations. Among additional functions of the skin, which one involves fibroblasts?
    a. Communication
    b. Healing wounds
    c. Thermoregulation
    d. Immune responses

75. For a new skincare client, what might be included on the Health History part of the Skincare History form that the practitioner asks the client to complete?
    a. Exercise
    b. Allergies
    c. Nutrition
    d. All of the above

76. Which of the following is true of drawbacks to shaving as a temporary hair removal method?
    a. It is abrasive and can irritate skin.
    b. It makes hairs grow back thicker.
    c. It is faster and more convenient.
    d. It needs hairs of a certain length.

77. What is a disadvantage of waxing as a method of removing hair temporarily?
    a. It lasts longer than depilation.
    b. It can be painful and irritate skin.
    c. It has lighter regrowth than depilation.
    d. It pulls out hairs rather than cutting them.

78. Which of the following is true about depilatory creams and lotions?
    a. They can irritate and darken skin like shaving.
    b. They remove hair by dissolving from the root.
    c. They use a non-chemical kind of hair removal.
    d. They deliver results as long-lasting as waxing.

79. In a salon that includes electrolysis/electrology services, this equipment must be...
    a. Sterilized by a sterilizer that uses only steam.
    b. Sterilized by a sterilizer approved by the FDA.
    c. Sterilized by a sterilizer that has only dry heat.
    d. Sterilized by a sterilizer using ultraviolet light.

80. Regarding the safety of ingredients in skincare products, which of the following is true?
    a. Public health laws regulate the use of most chemical ingredients.
    b. Public health laws require complete, accurate ingredient labeling.
    c. Public health laws permit unsubstantiated product benefit claims.
    d. Public health laws require safety testing of products' ingredients.

81. Which of the following is true about facial massage?
    a. It has no visible effect on wrinkles.
    b. It is not used to relieve puffy eyes.
    c It is relaxing but will not help acne.
    d. It can enhance the healing of skin.

82. People with ___ skin tone sunburn easily, have some ___ color, look better in ___ jewelry; ___-red lipstick brightens them up, and veins showing through their skin look ___. People with ___ skin tone tan easily; their skin has ___ undertones; they look better in ___ jewelry, look brighter with ___-red lipstick, and veins under their skin look ___.
    a. Warm; yellow; copper; orange; blue; cool; blue; silver; pink; blue
    b. Cool; green; silver; purple; green; warm; green; brass; blue; green
    c. Cool; pink; silver; blue; blue; warm; golden/yellow; gold; orange; green
    d. Warm; orange/yellow; silver; orange; green; cool; blue; gold; pink; blue-green

83. Which color family of eye shadows will make blue eyes look even bluer?
    a. Blues
    b. Browns
    c. Pinks
    d. Purples

84. Corrective makeup is needed least for...
    a. Sheer color.
    b. Rosacea.
    c. Vitiligo.
    d. Scars.

85. Which of the following is true about applying individual false eyelashes?
    a. An eyelash curler should only be used afterward.
    b. These look more natural than full strips of lashes.
    c. Mascara is used only after the lashes are applied.
    d. After applying a lash, press lightly with a fingertip.

Nail Care and Services

86. Which of the following is true about the growth of human fingernails and toenails?
    a. In humans, the toenails grow faster than fingernails.
    b. Fingernails grow at the same rates on all the fingers.
    c. Index fingernails grow faster than pinkie fingernails.
    d. Human nails grow at the same rate in every season.

87. Fingernail clubbing, wherein the fingertips enlarge and the nails curve around them, is...
    a. A harmless inherited condition.
    b. Due to causes that are unknown.
    c. Always a sign of one specific disease.
    d. Caused by several different diseases.

88. The germinal matrix of the human fingernail (or toenail) is also known as...
    a. The nail cuticle.
    b. The nail plate.
    c. The nail root.
    d. The nail bed.

89. Beau's lines refers to a condition of horizontal indentations on the fingernails. Which of the following is true about this condition?
    a. It cannot be caused by any kind of injury to the nail(s).
    b. It can be related to conditions affecting circulation.
    c. It can come from illnesses that do not cause fevers.
    d. It can be related to injury but not nutritional causes.

90. Which of these is true about vertical ridges in the fingernails?
    a. These are relatively common and no cause for concern.
    b. These are relatively unusual and should be investigated.
    c. These are nearly always signs of some underlying illness.
    d. These are inherited and not found to change with aging.

91. When whirlpool foot spas are included in the equipment used for giving pedicures, when must these be cleaned and disinfected?
    a. After each use with a client
    b. At all these times combined
    c. At the end of each workday
    d. After a period of two weeks

92. If cuticle nippers are used during a manicure, what should these be cutting away?
    a. The eponychium skin
    b. Lateral nail folds' skin
    c. Only the true cuticles
    d Nippers cut all of these

93. If using a cuticle pusher during a manicure, which of the following should the manicurist do?
    a. Press hard
    b. Press down
    c. Press down hard
    d. Never do any of these

94. What is/are included in the benefits of using warmed paraffin wax during some manicures and/or pedicures?
    a. It will deep condition the skin.
    b. It will moisturize skin that is dry.
    c. It provides all of these benefits.
    d. It relieves tired, sore hands/feet.

95. When are special precautions necessary for manicures or pedicures?
    a. They are necessary if the client has atherosclerosis, but not if the client has diabetes.
    b. They are necessary for any peripheral vascular diseases, blood thinners, and diabetics.
    c. They are necessary if the client takes prescription blood thinners but not daily aspirin.
    d. They are necessary only when the client brings in a written prescription from a doctor.

96. When giving a hand and arm massage during a manicure, what is true about a massage medium?
    a. It should be a lotion or oil dedicated for massage.
    b. Any kind of all-purpose oil or lotion may be used.
    c. It is best to avoid applying any kind of a medium.
    d. A medium can be used, but not rubbed into skin.

97. When giving a foot and leg massage, what does it mean to use cross-fiber friction on the heels?
    a. Pushing up on the heel with both thumbs and then down with both thumbs
    b. Pushing up on the heel with one thumb, while pushing down with the other
    c. Rubbing vigorously across the heels with both thumbs in opposite directions
    d. Rubbing across the heels with all fingers of each hand, in opposite directions

98. Which of the following is a recommended sequence for post-service procedures following client nail care?
    a. Record service information; advise the client about home maintenance; promote sales of suitable products; clean up the work area; disinfect all implements; schedule the client's next appointment.
    b. Advise the client about home maintenance; record service information; promote sales of suitable products; disinfect all implements; clean up the work area; schedule the client's next appointment.
    c. Schedule the client's next appointment; advise the client about home maintenance; promote sales of suitable products; clean up the work area; disinfect all implements; record service information.
    d. Clean up the work area; disinfect all implements; promote sales of suitable products; advise the client about home maintenance; record service information; schedule the client's next appointment.

99. What is true about factors that can lead to nail infection from having acrylic nails applied?
    a. Infections only occur when the acrylic nails are applied using unsanitary tools.
    b. A gap/separation between natural and acrylic nails does not cause infections.
    c. If the acrylic nails used are too rigid, it can cause discomfort but not infection.
    d. When the acrylic nails applied are too long, this can also cause a nail infection.

100. Which of the following is a correct statement about nail art?
    a. Nail art can be applied onto artificial nails but not natural nails.
    b. Most base coats are incompatible with nail art and unneeded.
    c. Nails should be trimmed and shaped first but not overly short.
    d. A top coat is unnecessary with nail art and can damage the art.

Answers and Explanations

Scientific Concepts

1. A: Sterilization kills all microbes and spores, and is the preferred method for instruments. Sanitizing (B) only reduces the number of microorganisms, and often only harmful ones rather than beneficial ones. Disinfection (C) can disable viruses and get rid of most but not all microbes, and will not eliminate their spores; it is mainly used for decontaminating the air and surfaces rather than instruments. Therefore, choice (D) is incorrect.

2. B: Certain hospital disinfectants are registered with the Environmental Protection Agency (EPA). Relative to cosmetology, the Food and Drug Administration or FDA (A) regulates cosmetics, soaps, and drugs used as personal care products. Relative to cosmetology, the Centers for Disease Control (CDC) and Prevention regulates permanent cosmetics, body piercing, tattoos, and related facilities. The Occupational Safety and Health Administration (OSHA) regulates the safety of storing, handling, using, controlling, transporting, and disposing of hazardous materials used in workplaces.

3. C: Vacuoles are the main storage units in human cells for water, food, and waste until these are utilized or eliminated. Mitochondria (A) are the cells' power sources that convert food nutrients into energy. Lysosomes (B) break down proteins, some fats, and sugars via chemical reactions. Nuclei (D) are the central "brains" of cells and contain RNA and DNA.

4. D: DNA (deoxyribonucleic acid) is the material that makes up a person's genetic building blocks. RNA (ribonucleic acid) is a messenger that makes "negative" copies of the DNA and transports them out of the cells' nuclei to the ribosomes so they can manufacture proteins. Plasma is the material of which the membranes containing human cells are made; cytoplasm is the material inside the cells that surrounds their organelles {(A), (B)}. Because option (D) is correct, option (C) is incorrect.

5. D: Epithelial tissue covers all outer and inner body surfaces and is the primary glandular tissue. It serves functions of secreting, excreting, absorbing, protecting, and perceiving sensory information. Connective (A) tissue, the most abundant in the body, binds together bodily structures and serves functions of filling space, protecting, supporting, creating a framework, storing fat, producing blood cells, repairing tissues, and fighting infections. Muscle (B) tissue serves functions of voluntary movement in the skeletal muscles and involuntary movement in hollow organs like the stomach and the heart. Nerve (C) tissue functions to transmit signals in the neurons (nerve cells) of the brain, and to protect and support the neurons in the neuroglia of the brain.

6. C: The heart pumps blood out to the body through the arteries. Blood comes back to the heart from the rest of the body through the veins. Both types of blood vessels carry blood rather than only containing it (A). Choice (B) is the reverse of the correct answer. Arteries carry blood from the heart and veins carry blood back to the heart, making option (D) incorrect.

7. B: The nose acts as a filter when people inhale through it by keeping out irritating particles. If irritants still reach the lungs, the mucus (A) lining the insides of the trachea and bronchi does not filter but rather traps them. The cilia (C), tiny hairs that also line the trachea and bronchi, do not filter but move the mucus from the lungs to the epiglottis, which opens to let people swallow the mucus. The cough (D) does not filter but moves mucus out of the lungs faster than the cilia can when necessary.

8. A: The epidermis, the outermost layer of the skin, contains the melanocytes. The subcutis (B), the innermost layer of the skin, contains fat cells and collagen. The dermis (C), the middle layer of the skin, contains sweat glands, hair follicles, blood and lymph vessels, fibroblasts, collagen bundles, and nerves. Therefore, choice (D) is incorrect because only the epidermis contains melanocytes.

9. A: The mandible is the lower jaw bone and is a single cranial bone. The lacrimal (B) bone is a paired bone; there is one on each side, at the inner corner of each eye (the root of *lacrimal* means "tears," and the lacrimal ducts are the tear ducts). The maxilla (C) is a paired bone; the two maxillae form the upper jaw, with one on each side of the face. The nasal (D) bones are also paired; together, they form the bridge of the nose.

10. B: The hyoid bone is located in the neck. It is closely related and important to the skull as it anchors muscles in the head, particularly the muscles of the tongue and the larynx. The frontal bone (A) is located within the skull at the front of the head, behind the forehead. The atlas (C) is the first cervical vertebra, which supports and balances the head atop the spinal column. The ossicles (D) are the tiny bones in the middle ear that vibrate in a chain to transmit sound to the inner ear, so these are also located within the skull.

11. C: The scapula, or shoulder blade, includes the acromion, coracoid process, and scapular spine. The clavicle (A) is the collarbone. It articulates with the scapula's acromion at one end but does not include this or the other processes. The humerus (B), classified as a shoulder bone, is in the upper arm and does not have these processes. The radius (D) is not classified as a shoulder bone but as an arm bone and is lower in the arm than the humerus.

12. D: The radius and ulna are the two bones in the lower arm or forearm. The humerus (A) is the upper-arm shoulder bone. The carpal and metacarpal (B) bones are respectively in the wrist and hand. The phalanges (C) are the bones in the fingers and thumb.

13. C: The seven bones in the ankle are the tarsals. The metatarsals (A) are the five bones in the instep of the foot, which connect to the tarsal bones. The calcaneus (B) is the heel bone in the foot. The phalanges (D) are the bones in the toes. ("Phalanges" is also the name for the finger and thumb bones.)

14. B: The lateral pterygoid muscle is the only chewing muscle that opens the jaw. The medial pterygoid (A) muscle closes and raises the jaw. The masseter muscle (C) closes the mouth and helps retract the mandible (lower jaw). The temporalis muscle (D) raises the mandible with its anterior (front) fibers and retracts the mandible with its posterior (back) fibers.

15. A: The tongue is itself a muscle and also contains muscles within it, covered with mucous membranes. It is also connected to four sets of muscles outside of it that anchor and move it in all directions. Therefore, choices (B), (C), and (D) are incorrect.

16. B: Vergence helps prevent double vision. The binocular vision of the human body's two eyes and their slightly different viewpoints is what gives people their three-dimensional perception. To keep this from becoming double vision, an inward turning of the eyes focuses images onto small parts of the retina with no rods. This movement is called vergence. During the movement, the brain gauges the degree of muscle tension to estimate the distances of objects viewed. Tremor (A) is a nearly imperceptible tremble when viewing a point of light in darkness and similar point images. Drift (C) is a natural off-center movement of viewed images, while flick (D) is a quick movement countering

drift by flicking the image back to the center. These coordinated movements prevent images from overwhelming vision receptors in any one place.

17. C: The dilatator naris anterior and dilatator naris posterior are the two nose muscles responsible for opening the nostrils. In normal breathing, they provide resistance against air pressure to keep the nostrils from closing. During some strong emotional reactions and/or labored breathing, they cause the nostrils to flare. The dyramidalis nasi (A), or procerus, muscle draws the eyebrows down over the bridge of the nose. The depressor septi (B) muscle opposes the other nose muscles and constricts the nostrils. The compressor naris (D), or nasalis, muscle depresses the nose cartilage and pulls the alar toward the septum.

18. D: The human hand has more than 60 different muscles, affording the hands a great variety and range of movement. Therefore, choices (A), (B), and (C) are incorrect by understating the number of muscles in the hand.

19. C: The human hand has thumbs that are opposed to the other four fingers, enabling them to write using implements, pick things up, make and build things, and many more. Most anthropologists believe that opposable thumbs have given humans the advantage over other animals for forming civilizations by making it possible to write down historical events, make tools, and create things with those tools. Disks in the wrists (A) enable humans to turn their hands 180 degrees down and up, i.e., pronate and supinate them. The thenar muscles (B) are small intrinsic hand muscles controlling the thumb side of the palm. Hypothenar muscles (D) are small intrinsic hand muscles controlling the pinky finger side of the palm.

20. B: Abductors are muscles that move the legs (and hips, arms, and digits) outward, while adductors move them inward. Flexors are muscles that cause body parts to contract or tighten, while extensors are muscles that cause them to stretch or extend {(C), (D)}.

21. A: The human shoulder joint is the most mobile joint in the whole body. Being the joint that is most free to move, it is more mobile than it is stable, rather than vice versa (B). While the shoulder joint is relatively strong, it is not stronger than it is mobile (C) because it is so highly moveable that it sacrifices stability and strength in favor of mobility. Its free movement makes it more susceptible to dislocation and other injuries. Because it is not a highly stable joint, it is also not more stable than strong (D).

22. B: The veins in the stomach and intestines carry blood to the liver via the hepatic portal vein. After the liver processes digestive products, stores sugars, and removes toxins from the blood, this blood is returned through the inferior vena cava to the heart (D). Blood is carried from the heart to the abdominal aorta and through the renal hilus to the kidneys (C) by the renal arteries. Blood is carried from the heart to the lungs (D) by the pulmonary arteries.

23. C: The pancreas is both an endocrine gland, producing hormones to regulate blood sugar; and an exocrine gland, secreting digestive enzymes to break down foods. The pituitary (A) gland is an endocrine gland, producing hormones to regulate growth, sexual development, reproduction, and metabolism. The thyroid (B) gland is an endocrine gland, producing hormones to regulate and convert nutrients into energy. The adrenal (D) glands are endocrine glands that produce hormones to break down proteins and fats and convert them to glucose, regulate mineral concentrations, regulate growth and activity in cells that receive male hormones, and support physiological stress responses. The endocrine system includes all of the body's glands. Only the pancreas also works as a digestive gland.

- 49 -

24. D: The hair (A), skin (B), and nails (C) are all parts of the integumentary system, which also includes the sweat (sudoriferous) glands, oil (sebaceous) glands, and ear wax (ceruminous) glands.

25. C: As waste filtered out of the blood, urine first is collected in the kidneys. It empties out of the kidneys through the ureters into the bladder. It then leaves the body by emptying out of the bladder through the urethra during urination.

26. B: Plasma is the fourth state of matter. It has no definite volume or shape, similar to gases (D); however, it is different from gas in that plasma conducts electricity because it has free electrical charges. Gases can be heated and ionized to create plasma. Solids (A) have definite shapes and volumes. Liquids (C) have definite volumes but not shapes. A liquid in a container fits into the container's shape.

27. A: Fat-soluble vitamins, like vitamin A, vitamin D, or vitamin E, can build up in the bloodstream to unsafe levels if consumed in excess; water-soluble vitamins, like vitamin C or any of the B-complex vitamins, can be broken down and excreted as waste by the body if consumed to excess. Choice (B) is the reverse of the correct answer. Dietary minerals (C) may be either bulk/quantity elements, like calcium, sodium, or potassium; or trace elements (D), like copper, iron, or zinc. Either type can also build up to unsafe levels in the blood if excessive amounts are ingested.

28. B: Compounds can only be broken down into their components through chemical reactions, whereas mixtures can be separated into their components through mechanical processes like evaporation, magnetism, or filtration. Choice (A) is the reverse of the correct answer. Compounds can only be created through chemical reactions, whereas mixtures can be created mechanically, rather than vice versa (C). The properties of compounds are different from the properties of their component parts; whereas the properties of mixtures are generally more similar to and dependent upon the properties of their ingredients, rather than the opposite (D).

29. D: Micro-current Electrical Neuromuscular Stimulation (MENS), or micro-current treatment, is popularly known as a nonsurgical facelift or facial lifting. It is used to rejuvenate the skin. It softens wrinkles, sun damage, acne scars, stretch marks, and cellulite. Galvanic treatment (A) cleanses and nourishes the skin by introducing a constant, small direct current. High-frequency treatment (B) applies low alternating currents with high frequencies to help heal the skin through warming, drying, and killing germs. It also exfoliates the skin and stimulates the oil glands and sweat glands. Neuromuscular electrical stimulation (NMES) or Faradic treatment (C) tones the muscles by introducing an interrupted, direct electrical current in short pulses to cause repeated muscle contractions.

30. D: The EPA's partner program called Design for the Environment (DfE) scientifically reviews various products (like cleaning products), screening each of the ingredients in every product for possible effects on both human health (B) and the environment (C). Products with the DfE label have been found to be safer for people to use and safer for the environment according to the EPA's rigorous standards. DfE labeling additionally identifies chemical products that are safer without sacrificing effectiveness (A).

Hair Care and Services

31. C: The part of a hair outside the skin is the hair shaft or fiber; the part under the skin is the hair root. The enlarged base of the hair root is the bulb. The bulb is encased in a pocket in the skin called the hair follicle. The follicle is nourished by a small, cone-shaped bump at its bottom called the dermal papilla.

32. B: Round hair follicles cause hairs to grow out of them straight, whereas oval hair follicles cause the hairs to grow out wavy or curly. (Follicles with more rounded oval shapes result in wavy hair; the longer and thinner the ovals of the follicles, the curlier the hair.) Choice (A) is the reverse of the correct answer. The size {(C), (D)} of the hair follicles determines density, which is how thick or fine the hairs are, rather than whether they are straight or wavy/curly.

33. A: Elasticity is how soft and flexible the hair is. Hydrogen bonds and water intake affect hair elasticity. If the hair is more elastic, this means it is getting enough protein and water. Even damaged hair is more elastic when it is wet. Porosity (B) is how well the hair retains moisture. Texture (C) is whether the hair is fine, medium, or coarse, depending on how thin or thick the individual hair shafts are. Density (D) is how many hairs are on a person's head. (A person can have thick, fine hair or thin, coarse hair, among others.)

34. B: Trichorrhexis nodosa, a hair disease, may be secondary to hypothyroidism or certain genetic syndromes, but is more often caused by environmental traumas like overexposure to chemicals, heat styling, brushing too hard, and more. It involves "nodes" or swellings on the hair shafts causing breakage. Loose anagen syndrome (A), considered inherited and/or related to other diseases, does not cause hair breakage but rather loose hair that falls out easily. It is most common in white, blonde-haired female children (also occurring less often in boys and adults with darker hair). Seborrheic dermatitis (C) is a skin disorder affecting the scalp. It does not cause hair breakage but itching, flaking, and temporary or permanent hair loss from the scalp. Folliculitis (D) is a hair disease that does not cause hair breakage but inflammation of hair follicles (not just on the scalp but anywhere on the body having hair follicles) which swell, creating painful red bumps. It is caused by bacterial infection or friction from shaving or clothing, and is usually resolved with topical antiseptics.

35. C: A short cut is good for straight, fine hair. However, the layers will not be as obvious as the client wants because layers of soft, fine hair blend together. Highlighting with a lighter color can make layers more visible; or styling, such as by curling, or "spiking" layers to stand out. While a blunt cut adds volume, longer styles are not always best for very fine hair (A) because the length can make it look even thinner and also make it less manageable. While a short cut with any hair type can make the head look smaller (B), this is not a reason to avoid it if the client's head and body are in proportion. This client's hair type will not naturally make layering stand out the most (D), but coloring/styling techniques as in option (C) can.

36. D: Most state agencies that license hairstylists require blade guards on razors when giving razor cuts during their licensure tests. The tests evaluate not only the candidate's hairstyling skills, but also his/her knowledge of the sanitation and safety protocols for cutting and styling hair. Most state licensing tests do not require the candidate to do razor cuts with and without blade guards (A), but only with them. Razor blades are very sharp and can easily cause injuries as well as haircutting accidents. A hairstylist DOES need experience to give good razor cuts (B). Haircutting experts advise clients against getting a razor cut from a stylist who is new at it. There are also stylists who

Copyright © Mometrix Media. You have been licensed one copy of this document for personal use only. Any other reproduction or redistribution is strictly prohibited. All rights reserved.

have many years of experience with doing razor cuts and would never do one without a blade guard on the razor (C).

37. C: Synthetic hair wigs generally have their styles already set, and shampooing them with cold water does not remove the style. Meanwhile, natural hair wigs must be restyled after washing, the same as a person's own real hair. Synthetic wigs are NOT as durable as natural hair wigs, and cannot be exposed to extreme heat (A). Natural hair wigs, like people's own hair, can be damaged or broken by excessive heat styling, but can tolerate heat from styling tools better than synthetic hair can. Natural hair wigs are MORE expensive than synthetic ones (B). While natural hair wigs can be colored with ordinary hair color the same as one's own hair, synthetic hair wigs cannot (D).

38. B: The average human hair on a young, healthy person grows about a half-inch in a month. Some individuals whose hair grows very fast might grow an inch in a month (A), but they are in the minority. For hair to grow only a quarter-inch a month (C) is a slower-than-normal rate. It is very rare for someone's hair to grow two inches in a month (D).

39. A: Each hair on a healthy person's head, under normal conditions, will last for from one to six years. Choices (B) and (C) are longer than the typical life of a hair, and choice (D) is much shorter than the usual life of a hair.

40. B: The most accurate statement of the reason for baldness is that no more new hairs are produced to replace the old hairs. All of the person's hair falling out (A) is not as accurate because normally, new hairs are produced and replace the old hairs by pushing them until they fall out as the new hairs grow from the roots. Old hairs falling out faster than usual (C) is not as accurate for the same reason: new hairs normally replace the old ones. New hairs falling faster than they typically do (D) is also not as accurate because as long as new hairs are being produced, there would still be some hair on the head because different hairs begin growing at different times.

41. C: Human hair grows at around the same speed on all parts of the head. Some people who wear bangs think these grow faster (A), but it just seems that way because when bangs are right above their eyebrows, the tiniest amount of new growth that needs trimming looks more obvious to them than growth elsewhere. Hair does not grow fastest on the crown (B) or the nape of the neck (D), either.

42. D: Dandruff is a different scalp condition than dry scalp (though the two are often confused), and is believed to be caused by infection. Dandruff can cause hair loss if not treated, whereas dry scalp (A) is not known to cause hair loss. Because option (A) is incorrect and option (D) is correct, options (B) and (C) are both incorrect.

43. C: People with oily scalp and long hair often complain that although daily shampooing removes the scalp oil, it also strips the ends of the hair, making them too dry. Yet they also find that using conditioner after daily shampooing makes the scalp oily again within only a few hours. Therefore they should not use both shampoo and conditioner from scalp to ends every day (A). Scalp astringents and oil-removing tonics will also strip the ends of the hair if allowed to run down from the scalp (B), so users should apply these with cotton balls to the scalp only. Shampooing daily without conditioner can leave the ends dry, and using shampoo plus conditioner less often can leave the scalp oily (D).

44. B: A final rinse with cool instead of warm water closes the pores in the skin of the scalp, slowing down the scalp's production of oil, which can benefit an oily scalp (A). A last rinse with cool water

also closes the cuticles of the hair shafts, making them lay flat so the hairs are smoother and appear shinier (C). This improves the look of dry, damaged, frizzy, or dull hair and generally benefits multiple hair types. While some people may find cool water following warm water uncomfortable, especially when the air is cold, it is not true that a cool rinse has no benefit (D).

45. A: Tinea capitis is also called ringworm of the scalp. It is caused by a fungus infecting the hair shafts. Trichotillomania (B) affects the hair but is not a scalp or hair disease; it is, rather, a mental health disorder wherein the patient compulsively pulls out his/her own hair. It is associated with obsessive-compulsive disorder, anxiety, and depression. Seborrheic dermatitis (C) is a skin disorder that affects the scalp as well as other areas, causing abnormally flaky and itchy skin. Its cause is unknown. The disease called folliculitis (D) is not a scalp disease but a hair disease, causing inflammation of the hair follicles anywhere on the skin, including the scalp. The inflammation results in red, painful bumps. Folliculitis is caused by bacterial infection or by friction from clothing or shaving.

46. B: Snap closures and Velcro closures on hair capes are about the same in terms of longevity. They both last long enough that the stitching in the cape is more likely to fray before the closures wear out. Thus, option (A) is not true. A main drawback to snaps is that if they break, they usually cannot be repaired. A main drawback to Velcro is that loose client hair attaches to it. This can interfere with the Velcro's grip as well as its appearance, and is also unsanitary. Also, removing hair from the Velcro is difficult and effortful, and can damage the Velcro's functioning. Snap closures give the hair cape a secure fit and are better for use with salon towels to protect the neck than with neck strips (C), while Velcro closures allow a more adjustable fit and are better for use with neck strips than with towels (D).

47. C: This is the only part of cape removal that is described correctly. Removing the cape quickly (A) will scatter loose hair all around to land on the client. Folding the back ends of the cape up and around the shoulders should be done first. Only after doing this should the stylist undo the cape's closure and remove the towel or neck strip (B). Then s/he should resume folding the cape up to enclose any loose hairs inside of it. After folding upward, the stylist should lift the cape horizontally away from the client, not vertically (D). All of these steps help to prevent the client from feeling itchy and looking messy with loose hairs on and in her/his clothes.

48. D: Astringent lotions, cleansing agents, and/or medicated products are used in scalp treatments for oily scalp and/or scalp acne to open up clogged pores, increase scalp circulation, get rid of excessive oil, and control the production of oil. Deep-conditioning creams (A) are used for dry scalp to moisturize and condition the skin and follicles. Hot oil treatments (B) are also used for dry scalp, as are heat therapies (C).

49. C: Fine hair should be washed with shampoo designed to add volume and body. After washing, lightweight anti-frizz products can be applied to smooth the curls without weighing them down and flattening fine hair. Heavier-weight products that control frizz will weigh down fine hair, preventing volume and fullness (A). It is not as effective to add volumizing products after washing (B). Unfortunately, shampoos do not combine volumizing and anti-frizz ingredients in one product (D) because these are opposite effects that work against each other.

50. B: Leave-in conditioners are usually rich in moisture but lightweight so they do not weigh down the hair. The spray-on kinds give more control in application, so they can be used on dry, flyaway ends while avoiding roots that tend to look greasy from conditioner. This is a common problem with combination (oily/dry) hair and fine hair. Rinse-through conditioners (A) are the commonest

kind, typically used after shampooing. They detangle the hair, smooth the cuticle, and protect hair from heat styling damage. Deep conditioning hair masques (C) are good treatments for adding and sealing in moisture to extremely and/or chronically dry hair. Protein pack repair conditioners (D) are good for damaged hair; they restore proteins in the hair's cortex to make it stronger and more elastic. They also make wet sets more effective and long-lasting.

51. A: To encourage hair ends to curve under, the stylist can undercut or reverse-layer the ends by cutting the ends underneath shorter, removing a lot of their bulk so the ends on top are easier to turn under; and then styling the ends with a round brush and blow-dryer, a curling iron with a large barrel, hot rollers, or a flatiron. This is easiest with straight hair. Very wavy (B) or curly hair (C) are harder to style this way because hair with the alternating directions of waves or curls can flip up at the ends depending on where they are in the wave/curl pattern. Humidity (D) also sabotages this styling by restoring the hair's natural wave or curl.

52. B: It is impossible to change the natural direction of hair's growth pattern where portions grow in different directions. Styling with a blow-dryer (A) will not do this. Other than drastic measures like surgery to reposition the part of the scalp involved, only chemical straightening will let someone style the hair to lie in a different direction than its natural one. This is not an unusual condition (C); it is very common for people to have sections of hair that grow in different directions. Therefore, that this never happens (D) is also not true.

53. C: With problem growth patterns, such as the "double crown" described, the stylist should make sure the layers in that area are long enough to bend the hair into a different direction that the client wants. Therefore, the layers should not be very short (A). Anytime the stylist is working against a natural growth pattern, s/he should NOT hold sections of hair tightly when cutting them (B), but should hold them with no tension at all; holding the hair tightly can cause the cut to be too short. This effect is magnified with curly or wavy hair (D). When cutting to compensate for a growth pattern, the stylist should always err on the side of leaving the hair too long rather than too short.

54. D: Coarse hair means the individual hairs are each bigger around, while dense hair means there are more individual hairs on the head. Fine hair means the individual hairs are smaller around, while thin hair means there are fewer individual hairs on the head. If the hairs are coarse, fewer of them are needed to make the head of hair look full (B), but not as full as if the head has more of them. If the hairs are fine but there are many of them, the greater density will make the head of hair look thick, even with fine-textured individual hairs (A), but not as thick as coarse and dense hair. Fine-textured hairs with lower density (C), i.e., a smaller number of finer hairs, would look the least full of all these combinations.

55. C: To make the client's overweight face appear longer and/or narrower, and thus more oval in shape, the bangs should be cut on an angle (B) or swept to the side (D). Blunt-cut bangs (A) create a horizontal line that makes the face look even wider than it already is.

56. B: The combination of climate, hair type, and lifestyle described would dictate a short, natural style for the least fussing with hair. A long, straight (A) style would require regular styling and products to straighten the waves and control frizz. While the client's hair is naturally wavy, wearing the hair long (B) would still require anti-frizz treatments to keep the loose waves smooth. Because the client's hair does not naturally curl tightly, styling short, wavy hair into tight curls (D) would require both anti-frizz products and styling with tiny rollers. Even a permanent, using tiny rods, would require additional regular treatment and styling to keep the hair from frizzing and preserve the curls in a hot, humid climate.

57. A: Elevation is one element of haircutting. The points of elevation are zero degrees (A), meaning the hairs point straight down toward the floor; 180 degrees (B), meaning the hairs are held straight up toward the ceiling (as with an up-do or a spiked hairstyle); or 90 degrees (C), meaning the hairs are held straight out to the sides, parallel to the floor and ceiling. These elevation degrees are the same regardless of where the hair grows from on the head, so choice (D) is incorrect.

58. B: The lowest elevation and lowest angle of cutting will produce a blunt cut with no layering. Raising either the elevation or the angle of cutting, or both of these, will create layers in the hair. While increasing either one will produce layers, cutting with both a higher elevation and at a higher angle will produce the most layers. Numerous variations on the almost limitless possible combinations of elevations and angles of cutting hair in different places on the head produce a multitude of different haircut styles.

59. C: Slithering or sliding is a technique of texturizing or thinning the hair that is classified as a type of smooth cutting. Smooth cutting can be done by pulling a razor tool along the length of a hair section to reduce bulk with a tapered pattern; or by pulling the slightly opened blades of the scissors or shears along the hair, which is called "slithering" or "sliding." The chipping method (A), weaving method (B), and the method of using thinning shears or scissors (D) are all classified as types of internal cutting to texturize and/or thin the hair.

60. D: The most common reason that some stylists nick themselves when using haircutting shears/scissors to texturize or thin hair is that they move both blades of the shears at the same time. This causes nicking particularly when using the chipping method (snipping random pieces of hair internally) or the point cutting type of end finishing (cutting into the ends). Nicking accidents are caused by improper shears manipulation more than by moving the blades too close to the other hand (A). Stylists can attain greater control over their shears, as well as cleaner cuts, by moving only the thumb by itself (B) and not the fingers; this ensures that they are moving only one of the blades (C) at a time.

61. C: When giving a blunt cut (i.e., all one length with no layering), the stylist should hold the hair to be cut with no tension at all. The hair should not be held tightly (A) or with even a little tension (B). Blunt cuts are intended to hang evenly. Placing any tension on the hair while cutting it can cause the ends to turn out uneven. This would require cutting more hair to get the ends even, and experienced stylists should know how common it is for women to complain that their hair has been cut too short. No tension should be used to hold the hair being cut, regardless of its length (D) before and/or after cutting.

62. B: While the kinds of layers created in a graduated haircut depend on the angle(s) and elevation(s) the stylist uses when cutting them, a long graduated haircut will generally have deeper layers, whereas a short graduated cut will have shallower layers, rather than the opposite (A). The length of the haircut does not dictate the number of layers {(C), (D)} as much as their length and/or spacing.

63. A: Fishtail braids are made using only two sections of hair instead of the three sections used to make basic braids, French braids, and cornrows. A rope braid is a variation on the French braid, so it is not completely distinct from any other braiding style (B). The rope braid features making a "twist" in the braid by flipping it over after each individual braiding. French braids and cornrows are not the same thing (C). French braids are made by adding more strands of hair into the braid as it progresses. Cornrows are tiny, very tight braids made by parting the hair into many small

- 55 -

sections. Basic braids involve only dividing the hair into three sections and crossing them, whereas French braids involve incorporating progressively more hair into the braid as it is made.

64. B: A full-cap wig has hair attached to a mesh base or cap that is elasticized. This kind of wig is usually hand-tied, which looks more natural; takes longer to make and is hence more expensive; and makes it easier to change parts and styles, especially when compared to a machine-tied wig. The full-cap wig is a better choice for someone who is bald or has very thin hair because its greater density covers the scalp better. Open-cap wigs (A) allow the scalp to show through between the wig's hair wefts. A cap-less wig (C) is simply another name for an open-cap wig. Because choice (B) is correct, choice (D) is incorrect.

65. C: It is very important to do a strand test of the client's hair before any chemical processing. For example, products giving "gradual" coverage to gray hairs typically use metallic salt dyes that cause a terrible reaction if the hair is subsequently treated with peroxide to bleach it or develop traditional hair coloring products: this can often totally melt the hair. Stylists should always do a preliminary test on a strand they have cut off of the client's hair, and especially when they are not sure what has been previously used on the hair. Strand testing is important to determine how long to leave a product on the hair, but this is not the only reason (A). It will show if a process will damage the hair; because some damage cannot be repaired (B), the process should not be used if testing shows damage. Strand tests are even more important when the client's hair is damaged, or a dramatic color change is proposed (D).

66. D: The chemical process of relaxing is the same as that of permanent waving, the only difference being that relaxing is used to remove curl while waving is used to add curl. The chemicals typically used in these processes (Ammonium Thioglycolate or other thiol compounds) are classified as hydroxides because they add hydrogen atoms to the sulfur atoms in the hair's disulfide bonds to break them. This process leaves the hair very alkaline, not acidic (A), even after rinsing thoroughly. To restore the hair to a normal pH—not moisturize (B) it—a neutralizing lotion or shampoo is used after relaxing (or perming). While the chemical process can definitely damage the hair, neutralizing/normalizing does NOT oxidize (C) because oxidizers can do even more severe damage to hair processed by hydroxides.

67. C: Mixing equal amounts of all colors will yield black. In terms of pigments like paint, hair color, and other substances (but not light itself), white (A) has no color. Brown (B) results from mixing equal amounts of two complimentary colors, like blue and orange, yellow and violet, or red and green. Gray (D) is really black with white added to it, making it lighter.

68. B: Semi-permanent hair color gets into the hair's cuticle but does not go deeper to the cortex. Demi-permanent hair color (C) has smaller color molecules, which not only penetrate the hair's cuticle but also go deeper into the hair's cortex. This makes it better for coloring gray hair. However, demi-permanent color's smaller molecules more easily come out of the hair's cuticle as well as going into it, so it fades over repeated shampoos. Permanent hair color (D) not only penetrates the cuticle and cortex of the hair, it also has ingredients that react with its hydrogen peroxide (bleach) to create larger color molecules, which stay inside the cortex rather than washing out like demi-permanent color's smaller molecules do.

69. A: Once hair has been colored, it tends to be more porous than virgin hair. Therefore, the color should be left on the hair a shorter time; colored hair is not more resistant than virgin hair (B), but less. At first, only new roots should be retouched to minimize hair damage and prevent previously colored hair from absorbing too much color. If all of the hair eventually needs recoloring, it is good

to condition the hair a few days in advance to protect it from damage and make it absorb color more easily so the color lasts longer. However, the conditioner used should NOT be a hot oil treatment (C) or protein-based (D) because these can keep color from saturating the hair fully. They can also strip color from the hair, so they should not be used right after coloring either.

70. B: Traditionally called a "soap cap," this method of lifting excessive color can be done several ways: Mix and apply equal amounts of 40-volume peroxide and either conditioner or shampoo and leave on, covered with a plastic cap, 20 minutes under low heat—using a bonnet-type hair dryer set on Low; a hand-held blow-dryer with the diffuser attachment; or by wrapping the plastic cap with towels warmed in a clothes dryer. Repeat this process until the color is lifted enough. Another method is applying the peroxide-and-shampoo mixture after washing hair, leaving it on only five minutes, rinsing thoroughly and conditioning the hair well, and repeating at each shampoo until the desired color is reached. This is gentler than bleaching and re-coloring (A) and takes less time than letting the hair grow out (C). Unless the hair is otherwise severely damaged, option (D) is not true.

Skin Care and Services

71. C: Itching is a function controlled by the skin's sensory nerve endings, which also regulate sensations of heat, cold, pain, pressure, and vibration. The skin's motor nerve endings control the functions of blood flow (A), sweating (B), and piloerection, which is when the hairs stand up (D) on the skin (a phenomenon sometimes known as "goose bumps").

72. D: The skin over the eyelids has an epidermal layer as thin as one-tenth of a millimeter. The epidermis of the skin over most of the body (A) is typically about a half-millimeter thick. The epidermis of the skin over the soles of the feet (B) and the palms of the hands (C) is the thickest; it has no sweat glands or hair follicles, and has a particularly strong, protective stratum corneum.

73. C: Cellulitis is a common infection of the skin, usually caused by staphylococcus (staph) or streptococcus (strep) bacteria. Lupus (A) and psoriasis (D) are autoimmune skin conditions caused by the body's own immune system. While the exact cause of vitiligo (B), which causes the skin to lose pigment, is unknown, it is also thought to be an autoimmune condition.

74. B: Fibroblasts are included in the skin's healing of wounds, along with basal layer cells in the epidermis and epidermal appendages. Activated by skin injuries, fibroblasts make new collagen to form scar tissue and eventually more normal skin. The communication (A) function involves blood flow, secretion of pheromones, and secretion of apocrine sweat. These communicate signals visually, as in blushing; through smell, as in body odor; and both, as in nervous perspiration. The function of thermoregulation (C), i.e., controlling how the body retains and dissipates heat, involves the sweat glands, blood flow, and hypodermal fat. The function of immune responses (D) involves the skin's immune cells: the Langerhans cells identify foreign antigens in the skin's epidermis, and the mast cells initiate inflammatory responses to skin damage.

75. D: The Health History portion of the Skincare History form that a new skincare client would complete typically includes whether or not the client exercises (A); has any allergies (B); takes nutritional (C) supplements; as well as genetic background, medications, medical conditions, and the name of the client's dermatologist and physician because all of these factors affect the condition of the skin as well as how the skin may react to various treatments.

76. A: As a temporary hair removal method, shaving is abrasive and can irritate the skin, particularly if the skin is sensitive. However, it is NOT true that shaving makes the hairs grow back thicker (B). Shaving cuts the hairs off bluntly above the skin, so as they grow back, they feel stiffer and coarser due to their blunt ends. This feeling is the source of the myth. Shaving is faster and more convenient (C) than many other temporary methods of hair removal; this is an advantage rather than a disadvantage. Another advantage of shaving is that the hairs need not grow to a certain length (D) to be removed, as other methods may require.

77. B: One disadvantage of waxing is that it can be a painful procedure and can irritate the skin. Waxing is classified as epilation, i.e., pulling the hairs out of their follicles, rather than depilation, i.e., cutting the hairs off (D) or dissolving them at the skin surface as with depilatory creams/lotions. Because the entire hair is pulled out, waxing lasts longer (A), an advantage rather than a disadvantage. The regrowth after waxing is also lighter than with shaving or depilatories (C), also an advantage.

78. A: Depilatory creams and lotions can irritate the skin as shaving can, and both can darken the skin in some individuals, particularly those with Asian ancestry. While they do not cut the hair like shaving, they use a chemical process of removing hair (C) and these chemicals can irritate some people's skin. Depilatories dissolve the hair at or just below the skin surface, but not from the root (B). These products deliver results about as short-lived as shaving, not as long-lasting as waxing (D) because waxing pulls the hair out while depilatories only dissolve it just below the skin surface at best.

79. B: Electrolysis/electrology equipment in salons must be sterilized using a sterilizer that is approved by and registered with the federal Food and Drug Administration (FDA). The sterilizer used may use either steam (A) or dry heat (C); both are acceptable. However, ultraviolet light sterilizers (D) are not enough for either sterilizing electrology equipment or disinfecting metal tools and instruments.

80. C: According to the Environmental Working Group, public health laws do not require manufacturers to prove or back up their claims about benefits of skincare products. These laws also permit personal care products to contain most chemicals as ingredients, rather than regulating their use (A). Public health laws do not require manufacturers to label their cosmetic products completely and accurately (B), so the product labels can be incomplete and/or misleading about the products' ingredients. Safety testing of cosmetic products and/or their ingredients is not required (D) by public health regulations.

81. D: Facial massage increases blood circulation. By stimulating the removal of lymph, stable blood, and waste products from the tissues, it makes room for fresh, more oxygenated blood. This brings more oxygen and more new red blood cells, which stimulate healing. Massage also relaxes the facial muscles and connective tissues, which softens the appearance of facial expression wrinkles (A). By reducing fluid buildup, it reduces puffiness around the eyes (B). In addition to being relaxing, facial massage helps to eliminate toxins that cause acne (C).

82. C: People with cool skin tones sunburn easily, have some pink (rosy) color, look better in silver jewelry, look brighter in blue-red (red with cool undertones) lipstick, and the veins under their skin look blue. People with warm skin tones tan easily, their skin has golden/yellow undertones, they look better in gold jewelry, look brighter with orange-red (red with warm undertones) lipstick, and the veins under their skin look green. (People with "neutral" skin tones have combinations of both

cool and warm undertones in their skin. They can wear both cool and warm colors, and their veins typically appear as blue-green.)

83. B: Eye color is enhanced by eye makeup in the eye's complimentary color, or close to it. While the complimentary color of blue is orange, this can be a difficult color in eye shadow as it does not always flatter the skin color, especially fair skin with cool undertones, which is more common in people with blue eyes. Browns, taupes, tans, and other colors in the brown family are a good solution. The orange (the combination of yellow and red) in them brings out the blue of the eyes, while the touch of blue that makes them more brown than orange cools the color down to harmonize better with skin tones. Conversely, blues (A) in eye shadows will bring out the color of brown and hazel-brown eyes. Pinks (C) will bring out the color of green eyes (pink is a tint of red, the compliment of green). Purples (D) likewise flatter green eyes; purple is a blend of pink/red and blue.

84. A: Anyone who wants sheer (or transparent, "see-through") coverage does not need corrective makeup. Usually, a light tinted moisturizer is enough to give some sheer color. Corrective makeup typically offers much fuller coverage to camouflage skin problems. Some of these problems may be caused by rosacea (B), a skin disease that causes redness and broken/enlarged capillaries (and sometimes red bumps, and pimples in some cases); vitiligo (C), a skin disease that causes loss of pigment resulting in white patches; and scars (D) from acne, injury, or surgery. Corrective makeup gives a finish that is opaque (yet also natural-looking in high-quality products) to cover such skin blemishes, and can even hide tattoos.

85. B: For those who find the appearance of full strips of false eyelashes unnatural or overdone, individual lashes applied one at a time give a more natural look. An eyelash curler should be used before applying (A) to give the natural eyelashes a bend, which helps them blend better with the false lashes. It also prepares natural and false lashes to blend better by applying one coat of mascara to the natural lashes before applying the false lashes (C). (Lightly running a mascara wand through all lashes after applying the false ones is also good for blending and making them point in the same direction.) After dipping a lash into a tiny dot of adhesive and placing it into the lash line with tweezers, it is better to press the false lash lightly onto the eyelid using the base (not points) of the tweezers rather than a fingertip (D) because skin oils in the fingertips can pull off the false eyelashes.

Nail Care and Services

86. C: Human nail growth corresponds to the length of the terminal phalange, i.e., the last finger or toe bone where the nail is located. Therefore, human fingernails grow faster than toenails, not vice versa (A); fingernails can grow up to four times as fast as toenails. Because nail growth is associated with bone length, the nails on longer fingers grow faster than on the little fingers rather than their all growing at the same rates (B). Season also affects nail growth, with summer being the season of the fastest growth; so nails do not grow at the same rate in every season (D). Genetics, age, gender, diet, and exercise also affect nail growth rates.

87. D: Clubbing of the fingernails, which usually develops gradually over a number of years, can be secondary to low blood oxygen resulting from different kinds of lung diseases. It can also be related to cardiovascular (heart and blood vessel) disease, liver disease, inflammatory bowel disease, and the AIDS virus. As such, it is not a harmless or inherited phenomenon (A) but should be investigated as it is a sign of some kind of disease, as it is associated with known disease conditions and is not

- 59 -

caused by unknown factors (B). As a number of different diseases can cause nail clubbing, it is not always a sign of one specific disease (C).

88. C: The germinal matrix of the nail is also called the nail root; it is under the skin behind the nail and produces most of the nail. The nail's cuticle (A) is also called the eponychium and is located between the nail and the skin of the finger or toe at the sides and base of the nail. The nail plate (B) is a name for the actual nail itself. The nail bed (D) is also called the sterile matrix and is located between the lunula ("moon"), i.e., the edge of the germinal matrix, and the hyponychium, i.e., the junction of the nail's free edge and the skin on the fingertip or toe tip.

89. B: Beau's lines can be related to untreated diabetes and to peripheral vascular disease, both conditions that affect the circulation. It can also be caused by injury (A) that interrupts nail growth underneath the cuticle. Beau's lines can be secondary to illnesses that cause high fevers (C), including measles, mumps, pneumonia, and scarlet fever. Additionally, Beau's lines can result from a zinc deficiency, so this condition can be related to nutritional causes (D).

90. A: Vertical ridges in the fingernails, running from the cuticles to the nail tips, are relatively common and are no cause for concern. Therefore, they are not unusual and do not need to be investigated (B). (Only horizontal nail ridges warrant medical examination.) Vertical nail ridges are not known to be signs of any underlying illness (C), as horizontal nail ridges can often be. Vertical ridges in the nails are NOT known to be inherited; but they ARE found to change with aging (D), often increasing in prominence and/or number. These changes are thought by some doctors to be caused by age-related changes to the cellular regeneration processes in the nails.

91. B: Whirlpool foot spas in salons can easily transmit microorganisms; there are reports of clients having caught bacterial infections that left permanent scars on their legs from using this equipment when it was not properly cleaned and disinfected. Therefore, regulations require salon operators to clean and disinfect each foot spa after each client use (A), at the end of each workday (C), and also every other week (D). Operators are also required to record the date and time when they clean and disinfect foot spas, and whether each cleaning and disinfection was a daily or a bi-weekly one. They are further required to make these records available to clients, and to representatives of the Board of Barbering and Cosmetology, whenever they request to see them.

92. C: When using cuticle nippers during a manicure, the manicurist should only cut the true cuticles of the nails. They should NOT cut the eponychium's live skin (A) or the live skin of the lateral nail folds (B). Nipping live skin can cause injury, bleeding, and infection. Practitioners with less experience using these implements should use cuticle nippers with the smallest cutting surface available (e.g., a quarter jaw rather than a half jaw or full jaw). Cuticle nippers should be used only to remove excess cuticle tissue and nothing else.

93. D: If using a cuticle pusher, the manicurist should NEVER press hard (A), press downward (B), or both (C) when pushing cuticles back because using too much pressure can damage the matrix of the nail. This kind of damage cannot be corrected and requires the entire nail to grow out completely before it will be normal again.

94. C: Paraffin wax warmed in a machine designed for this use offers multiple benefits to clients' hands and feet during manicures and pedicures. The wax provides deep conditioning (A) and moisturizing (B) of dry and damaged skin. It also brings relief to hands and feet that are tired, sore (D) and stressed. Practitioners can also use certain paraffin waxes that include added eucalyptus

and/or other essential oils to enhance the healing, soothing, and refreshing properties of the wax treatments.

95. B: Practitioners need to take special precautions when giving manicures and/or pedicures to clients who have diabetes, atherosclerosis or any other kind of peripheral vascular disease, and/or take daily medications that thin the blood—including aspirin. A written doctor's prescription is not required for the practitioner to take special precautions (D). While the client should inform the practitioner of any of these conditions, it is good for the practitioner to ask the client about them because some clients may forget or not realize they should tell the practitioner.

96. A: Experts recommend using a medium for hand and arm massage, and it should be an oil or lotion that is dedicated for use during massage rather than any all-purpose product (B). The medium reduces friction, so applying one should not be avoided (C). The practitioner should rub the medium into the client's skin (D) at the beginning of the massage to blend it into the skin surface.

97. B: Using cross-fiber friction on the heels is done by pushing up on the heel with one thumb while pushing down on it with the other thumb. Each thumb should be pushing the opposite way from the other, and thumbs can be alternated as long as one pushes up while the other pushes down. Both thumbs should not push down or up at the same time (A). Cross-fiber friction refers to pressing, not rubbing the heels, either with thumbs (C) or fingers (D).

98. C: After a manicure, the practitioner should first schedule the day, time, and type(s) of services for the client's next appointment, entering these in the appointment record and giving them to the client on an appointment card. Then s/he should advise the client about how to maintain the service results properly at home until the next appointment. The practitioner can then recommend products to the client that are appropriate for his/her needs. Once all post-service procedures directly involving the client are completed, the practitioner can then clean the work area and disinfect all tools used. Then the operator should record which services were performed, any observations, and any recommendations of specific products, in the client's record. Clients should not be kept waiting while operators clean the area, disinfect tools, or keep records. The operator should secure repeat business by scheduling the next appointment before selling products to the client or giving home maintenance advice.

99. D: Applying acrylic nails that are too long can lead to nail infection. Another thing that can cause nail infection to develop is applying acrylic nails that are too rigid (C). Nail infections can also occur if a gap or separation between the natural and acrylic nails develops (B), creating a warm, moist area that is hospitable to the growth of bacteria. Using unsanitary tools to apply acrylic nails can certainly cause nail infections, but this is not the only reason (A) because all of the above named factors can also lead to infections of the nails.

100. C: Nails should be trimmed and shaped before applying nail art, but they should not be made too short because the bigger the surface area of the nail, the more space there is to work with in creating the nail art. Nail art can be applied on artificial nails or natural nails (A), as long as they are protected by a base coat. Base coats are not incompatible with nail art or unneeded (B): a base coat protects nails from damage and/or stains from paints, bright/dark polish colors, and other materials used in nail art. The base coat also helps art and polish to stay on longer and not chip so soon. A clear top coat is recommended to protect the art and make it last longer. As long as every coat dries completely before applying the next one, a top coat will not damage the art (D).